POETS OF OUR TIME

POETS
OF
OUR
TIME

AN ANTHOLOGY COMPILED BY

F E S Finn BA

John Murray 50 Albemarle Street London W1

Printed in Hong Kong by
Dah Hua Printing Press Co., Ltd.

Limp 0 7195 0440 6
Paperback 0 7195 3243 4

The cover design on the limp edition is taken
from the painting *Gotha* by Victor Vasarely

Contents

JOHN BETJEMAN

Introduction   1
Upper Lambourne   3
Greenaway   3
Bristol and Clifton   4
In Westminster Abbey   6
Sunday Morning, King's Cambridge   7
The Village Inn   8
Diary of a Church Mouse   9
Christmas   11
London, from *Summoned by Bells*   12

CHARLES CAUSLEY

Introduction   17
King's College Chapel   19
The Seasons in North Cornwall   19
Keats at Teignmouth   20
Innocent's Song   20
At Grantchester   21
For an Ex-Far East Prisoner of War   21
Song of the Dying Gunner A.A.1.   22
Chief Petty Officer   22
Convoy   24
At the British War Cemetery, Bayeux   24
Death of an Aircraft   25
Cowboy Song   27
My Friend Maloney   28
Nursery Rhyme of Innocence and Experience   29
The Ballad of Charlotte Dymond   31

PATRIC DICKINSON

Introduction   35
Jodrell Bank   37

PATRIC DICKINSON (*cont'd*)

    The Onset   37
    On Dow Crag   38
    Bluebells   39
    The Scale of Things   39
    The Redwing   40
    The Dam   41
    Common Terns   42
    The Royal Military Canal   43
    The Roman Wall   45
    Heartbreak House   46
    Lines for an Eminent Poet and Critic   46
    Geologic   46
    Lament for the Great Yachts   47

CLIFFORD DYMENT

    Introduction   49
    The Carpenter   52
    Holidays in Childhood   53
    Fox   54
    A Switch Cut in April   54
    The Swans   55
    The Winter Trees   55
    Coming of the Fog   56
    The Dark City   56
    Bahnhofstrasse   56
    'From Many a Mangled Truth a War is Won'   57
    The Axe in the Wood   57
    Carrion   58
    Man and Beast   58
    The King of the Wood   59
    'Savage the Daylight and Annihilate Night'   60
    The Desert   60
    The Raven   61

TED HUGHES

    Introduction   63
    Bayonet Charge   65
    Griefs for Dead Soldiers   65

TED HUGHES (*cont'd*)

    Six Young Men   67
    Roarers in a Ring   68
    Dick Straightup   69
    The Jaguar   70
    The Horses   71
    Hawk Roosting   72
    Thrushes   73
    Pike   74
    View of a Pig   75
    Esther's Tomcat   76
    November   77
    Song   78

JAMES KIRKUP

    Introduction   81
    Seven Pictures from China:
        v *Landscape*   85
       VII *Autumn Grove after Rain*   85
    Sakunami   86
    Ghosts, Fire, Water   88
    No More Hiroshimas   89
    Earthquake   90
    The Submerged Village   91
    The Bowl of Goldfish: A Fable   93
    A City of the North   95
    A Visit to Brontëland   96
    To the Ancestral North   97
    For the 90th Birthday of Sibelius   98
    Rugby League Game   99
    To an Old Lady Asleep at a Poetry Reading   100
    Tea in a Space-Ship   101
    The Shepherd's Tale   101
    A Charm for the Ear-Ache   103

LAURIE LEE

    Introduction   105
    My Many-Coated Man   107
    Sunken Evening   107

LAURIE LEE (*cont'd*)

Bombay Arrival	108
Scot in the Desert	109
Home from Abroad	109
Seafront	110
The Long War	110
April Rise	111
The Three Winds	111
Field of Autumn	112
Apples	113
Stork in Jerez	113
Town Owl	114
Cock-Pheasant	115
Christmas Landscape	115

NORMAN NICHOLSON

Introduction	117
The Undiscovered Planet	119
The Expanding Universe	119
Gathering Sticks on Sunday	120
For the New Year	120
Cleator Moor	121
Bond Street	122
South Cumberland, 10th May 1943	123
South Cumberland, 16th May 1943	123
Five Minutes	124
Old Man at a Cricket Match	124
Michaelmas	125
The Pot Geranium	125
The Crocus	126
August	127
Innocents' Day	127
Windscale	128

ALAN ROSS

Introduction	129
Night Patrol	131
Survivors	132
Iceland in Wartime	132

ALAN ROSS (*cont'd*)

    Cricket at Brighton   133
    Winter Boats at Brighton   134
    North London   134
    Embankment before Snow   135
    Rock Paintings, Drakensberg   136
    Algerian Refugee Camp, Aïn-Khemouda   137
    Bantu on a Bicycle   137
    Nelson at Palermo   138
    Agrigento   139
    Grand Canal   140
    Winter Gulls   140

R. S. THOMAS

    Introduction   141
    Too Late   143
    Lament for Prytherch   143
    Servant   144
    A Welsh Testament   144
    Welsh History   146
    Welsh Landscape   146
    Looking at Sheep   147
    On the Farm   148
    The Muck Farmer   148
    The Labourer   149
    The Poacher   149
    Affinity   150
    Autumn on the Land   150
    The View from the Window   151
    A Blackbird Singing   151
    Pisces   152
    Poetry for Supper   152

    Sources and Acknowledgments   153

    Index of First Lines   157

John Betjeman

In his book, *John Betjeman*, Derek Stanford writes:

'In a time of consciously erudite poems, Mr Betjeman's poetry looks, at first sight, easy and simple stuff. The substance of any one poem by him is nearly always accessible without any special knowledge; but, in many instances, enjoyment and meaning is increased by a reference which might have escaped us, and which, in its unpretentious way, is as "learned" as any reference in more bookish poets. Allusions in modern verse are generally to the verse of the past. The culture of contemporary poetry is almost exclusively literary, and success in interpreting a poem aright comes from the reader's own breadth of reading. But this literary, or humanistic, culture is —one too often forgets—only a single feature in any way of living. No less a literary and allusive poet than T. S. Eliot reminds us of "just how much is . . . embraced by the term *culture*". "It includes," he tells us, "all the characteristic activities and interests of a people: Derby Day, Henley Regatta, Cowes, the twelfth of August, a cup final, the dog races, the pin table, the dart board, Wensleydale cheese, boiled cabbage cut into sections, beetroot in vinegar, nineteenth-century Gothic churches, and the music of Elgar. The reader," concludes Mr Eliot, "can make his own list," and Mr Betjeman, while subscribing to certain enthusiasms specified here, has also added some favourites of his own. "I love," he writes, "suburbs and gas-lights and Pont Street and Gothic Revival Churches and mineral railways, provincial towns and garden cities," and there are plenty of other likes and dislikes to be discovered in his work.

'Allusion, then, in Mr Betjeman's work is to this more popular body of interests and activities. One would need, for example, to be a keen gardener to appreciate fully all the many mentions of flowers, trees, and shrubs in his verse; and something of a sociologist, too, for Mr Betjeman's flowers have the look of "flowers that are looked at" and are emblems of class as well as of beauty.

'One needs, too, some general knowledge of the geography of social tone; a discerning eye for certain class-styles, as well as a "period" sense reaching back at least to the 1890's. Then, too, Mr. Betjeman is both time-table- and map-minded. He has impregnated with precarious magic the railway lines of London and the Home Counties. His verse has likewise awakened us to a new appreciation of all those churches dotted or hidden throughout the land; churches which we pass and never look at, or, looking at, still somehow fail to see.'

Mr Betjeman recalls a world which is disappearing, to be replaced by a new 'order': 'The roads slide with motor cars, the chasms are blue with petrol fumes, the sky roars with aeroplanes, deadly insects whose drone is like a dentist's drill in the brain; the pavements belch with the noise of radio shops, the public passages are too narrow, the public faces too pinched, the public food too inedible, the public mind too frightened; a ticket for this, a form for that, a set opinion about this, a standard dream of the unattainable. No wonder we lose our heads, no wonder we escape into the past.'

In a letter to the compiler of this anthology Mr Betjeman writes of his poems: 'My verse is made to be said out loud. I regard verse as the shortest and most memorable way of saying things—or rather that is what I think it ought to be. I also prefer to use rhythm and traditional forms as I think that until you know and can use rhyme and metre, you cannot know from what you are breaking free to write "free verse", nor distinguish between poetry and prose. I think verse is natural to all of us and is only killed by "Eng. Lit.". Nursery rhymes are what we all first know, and later, all sorts of people who never read poetry nevertheless know hundreds of popular songs by heart.'

UPPER LAMBOURNE

Up the ash-tree climbs the ivy,
    Up the ivy climbs the sun,
With a twenty-thousand pattering
    Has a valley breeze begun,
Feathery ash, neglected elder,
    Shift the shade and make it run—

Shift the shade toward the nettles,
    And the nettles set it free
To streak the stained Carrara headstone
    Where, in nineteen-twenty-three,
He who trained a hundred winners
    Paid the Final Entrance Fee.

Leathery limbs of Upper Lambourne,
    Leathery skin from sun and wind,
Leathery breeches, spreading stables,
    Shining saddles left behind—
To the down the string of horses
    Moving out of sight and mind.

Feathery ash in leathery Lambourne
    Waves above the sarsen stone,
And Edwardian plantations
    So coniferously moan
As to make the swelling downland,
    Far-surrounding, seem their own.

GREENAWAY

I know so well this turfy mile,
    These clumps of sea-pink withered brown,
The breezy cliff, the awkward stile,
    The sandy path that takes me down

To crackling layers of broken slate
    Where black and flat sea-woodlice crawl
And isolated rock pools wait
    Wash from the highest tides of all.

I know the roughly blasted track
   That skirts a small and smelly bay
And over squelching bladderwrack
   Leads to the beach at Greenaway.

Down on the shingle safe at last
   I hear the slowly dragging roar
As mighty rollers mount to cast
   Small coal and seaweed on the shore,

And spurting far as it can reach
   The shooting surf comes hissing round
To leave a line along the beach
   Of cowries waiting to be found.

Tide after tide by night and day
   The breakers battle with the land
And rounded smooth along the bay
   The faithful rocks protecting stand.

But in a dream the other night
   I saw this coastline from the sea
And felt the breakers plunging white
   Their weight of waters over me.

There were the stile, the turf, the shore,
   The safety line of shingle beach
With every stroke I struck the more
   The backwash sucked me out of reach.

Back into what a water-world
   Of waving weed and waiting claws?
Of writhing tentacles uncurled
   To drag me to what dreadful jaws?

BRISTOL AND CLIFTON

'Yes, I was only sidesman here when last
You came to Evening Communion.
But now I have retired from the bank
I have more leisure time for church finance.
We moved into a somewhat larger house
Than when you knew us in Manilla Road.
This is the window to my lady wife.

You cannot see it now, but in the day
The greens and golds are truly wonderful.'

'How very sad. I do not mean about
The window, but I mean about the death
Of Mrs. Battlecock. When did she die?'

'Two years ago when we had just moved in
To Pembroke Road. I rather fear the stairs
And basement kitchen were too much for her—
Not that, of course, she did the servants' work—
But supervising servants all the day
Meant quite a lot of climbing up and down.'
'How very sad. Poor Mrs. Battlecock.'
' "The glory that men do lives after them"
And so I gave this window in her name.
It's executed by a Bristol firm;
The lady artist who designed it, made
The figure of the lady on the left
Something like Mrs. Battlecock.'
'How nice.'

        'Yes, was it not? We had
A stained glass window on the stairs at home,
In Pembroke Road. But not so good as this.
This window is the glory of the church
At least I think so—and the unstained oak
Looks very chaste beneath it. When I gave
The oak, that brass inscription on your right
Commemorates the fact, the Dorcas Club
Made these blue kneelers, though we do not kneel:
We leave that to the Roman Catholics.'
'How very nice, indeed. How very nice.'

'Seeing I have some knowledge of finance
Our kind Parochial Church Council made
Me People's Warden, and I'm glad to say
That our collections are still keeping up.
The chancel has been flood-lit, and the stove
Which used to heat the church was obsolete.
So now we've had some radiators fixed
Along the walls and eastward of the aisles;
This last I thought of lest at any time
A Ritualist should be inducted here
And want to put up altars. He would find

The radiators inconvenient.
Our only ritual here is with the Plate;
I think we make it dignified enough.
I take it up myself, and afterwards,
Count the Collection on the vestry safe.'
'Forgive me, aren't we talking rather loud?
I think I see a woman praying there.'
'Praying? The service is all over now
And here's the verger waiting to turn out
The lights and lock the church up. She cannot
Be Loyal Church of England. Well, good-bye.
Time flies. I must be going. Come again.
There are some pleasant people living here.
I know the Inskips very well indeed.'

IN WESTMINSTER ABBEY

Let me take this other glove off
    As the *vox humana* swells,
And the beauteous fields of Eden
    Bask beneath the Abbey bells.
Here, where England's statesmen lie,
Listen to a lady's cry.

Gracious Lord, oh bomb the Germans.
    Spare their women for Thy Sake,
And if that is not too easy
    We will pardon Thy Mistake.
But gracious Lord, whate'er shall be,
Don't let anyone bomb me.

Keep our Empire undismembered
    Guide our Forces by Thy Hand,
Gallant blacks from far Jamaica,
    Honduras and Togoland;
Protect them Lord in all their fights,
And, even more, protect the whites.

Think of what our Nation stands for,
    Books from Boots' and country lanes,
Free speech, free passes, class distinction,
    Democracy and proper drains.
Lord, put beneath Thy special care
One-eighty-nine Cadogan Square.

Although, dear Lord, I am a sinner,
   I have done no major crime;
Now I'll come to Evening Service
   Whensoever I have the time.
So, Lord, reserve for me a crown,
And do not let my shares go down.

I will labour for Thy Kingdom,
   Help our lads to win the war,
Send white feathers to the cowards
   Join the Women's Army Corps,
Then wash the Steps around Thy Throne
In the Eternal Safety Zone.

Now I feel a little better,
   What a treat to hear Thy Word,
Where the bones of leading statesmen,
   Have so often been interr'd.
And now, dear Lord, I cannot wait
Because I have a luncheon date.

SUNDAY MORNING, KING'S CAMBRIDGE

File into yellow candle light, fair choristers of King's
   Lost in the shadowy silence of canopied Renaissance stalls
In blazing glass above the dark glow skies and thrones and wings
   Blue, ruby, gold and green between the whiteness of the walls
And with what rich precision the stonework soars and springs
   To fountain out a spreading vault—a shower that never falls.

The white of windy Cambridge courts, the cobbles brown and dry,
   The gold of plaster Gothic with ivy overgrown,
The apple-red, the silver fronts, the wide green flats and high,
   The yellowing elm-trees circled out on islands of their own—
Oh, here behold all colours change that catch the flying sky
   To waves of pearly light that heave along the shafted stone.

In far East Anglian churches, the clasped hands lying long
   Recumbent on sepulchral slabs or effigied in brass
Buttress with prayer this vaulted roof so white and light and strong
   And countless congregations as the generations pass
Join choir and great crowned organ case, in centuries of song
   To praise Eternity contained in Time and coloured glass.

THE VILLAGE INN

'The village inn, the dear old inn,
So ancient, clean and free from sin,
True centre of our rural life
Where Hodge sits down beside his wife
And talks of Marx and nuclear fission
With all a rustic's intuition.
Ah, more than church or school or hall,
The village inn's the heart of all.'
So spake the brewer's P.R.O.,
A man who really ought to know,
For he is paid for saying so.
And then he kindly gave to me
A lovely coloured booklet free.
'Twas full of prose that sang the praise
Of coaching inns in Georgian days,
Showing how public-houses are
More modern than the motor-car,
More English than the weald or wold
And almost equally as old,
And run for love and not for gold
Until I felt a filthy swine
For loathing beer and liking wine,
And rotten to the very core
For thinking village inns a bore,
And village bores more sure to roam
To village inns than stay at home.
And then I thought I *must* be wrong,
So up I rose and went along
To that old village alehouse where
In neon lights is written 'Bear'.

Ah, where's the inn that once I knew
    With brick and chalky wall
Up which the knobbly pear-tree grew
    For fear the place would fall?

Oh, that old pot-house isn't there,
    It wasn't worth our while;
You'll find we have rebuilt 'The Bear'
    In Early Georgian style.

But winter jasmine used to cling
    With golden stars a-shine

Where rain and wind would wash and swing
    The crudely painted sign.

And where's the roof of golden thatch?
    The chimney-stack of stone?
The crown-glass panes that used to match
    Each sunset with their own?

Oh now the walls are red and smart,
    The roof has emerald tiles.
The neon sign's a work of art
    And visible for miles.

The bar inside was papered green,
    The settles grained like oak,
The only light was paraffin,
    The woodfire used to smoke.

And photographs from far and wide
    Were hung around the room:
The hunt, the church, the football side,
    And Kitchener of Khartoum.

Our air-conditioned bars are lined
    With washable material,
The stools are steel, the taste refined,
    Hygienic and ethereal.

Hurrah, hurrah, for hearts of oak!
    Away with inhibitions!
For here's a place to sit and soak
    In sanit'ry conditions.

DIARY OF A CHURCH MOUSE

Here among long-discarded cassocks,
Damp stools, and half-split open hassocks,
Here where the Vicar never looks,
I nibble through old service books.
Lean and alone I spend my days
Behind this Church of England baize.

I share my dark forgotten room
With two oil-lamps and half a broom.
The cleaner never bothers me,
So here I eat my frugal tea.
My bread is sawdust mixed with straw;
My jam is polish for the floor.
   Christmas and Easter may be feasts
For congregations and for priests,
And so may Whitsun. All the same,
They do not fill my meagre frame.
For me the only feast at all
Is Autumn's Harvest Festival,
When I can satisfy my want
With ears of corn around the font.
I climb the eagle's brazen head
To burrow through a loaf of bread.
I scramble up the pulpit stair
And gnaw the marrows hanging there.
   It is enjoyable to taste
These items ere they go to waste,
But how annoying when one finds
That other mice with pagan minds
Come into church my food to share
Who have no proper business there.
Two field mice who have no desire
To be baptised, invade the choir.
A large and most unfriendly rat
Comes in to see what we are at.
He says he thinks there is no God
And yet he comes . . . it's rather odd.
This year he stole a sheaf of wheat
(It screened our special preacher's seat),
And prosperous mice from fields away
Come in to hear the organ play,
And under cover of its notes
Ate through the altar's sheaf of oats.
A Low Church mouse, who thinks that I
Am too papistical, and High,
Yet somehow doesn't think it wrong
To munch through Harvest Evensong,
While I, who starve the whole year through,
Must share my food with rodents who
Except at this time of the year
Not once inside the church appear.

Within the human world I know
Such goings-on could not be so,
For human beings only do
What their religion tells them to.
They read the Bible every day
And always, night and morning, pray,
And just like me, the good church mouse,
Worship each week in God's own house.
    But all the same it's strange to me
How very full the church can be
With people I don't see at all
Except at Harvest Festival.

CHRISTMAS

The bells of waiting Advent ring,
    The Tortoise stove is lit again
And lamp-oil light across the night
    Has caught the streaks of winter rain
In many a stained-glass window sheen
From Crimson Lake to Hooker's Green.

The holly in the windy hedge
    And round the Manor House the yew
Will soon be stripped to deck the ledge,
    The altar, font and arch and pew,
So that the villagers can say
'The church looks nice' on Christmas Day.

Provincial public-houses blaze
    And Corporation tramcars clang,
On lighted tenements I gaze
    Where paper decorations hang,
And bunting in the red Town Hall
Says 'Merry Christmas to you all.'

And London shops on Christmas Eve
    Are strung with silver bells and flowers
As hurrying clerks the City leave
    To pigeon-haunted classic towers,
And marbled clouds go scudding by
The many-steepled London sky.

And girls in slacks remember Dad,
    And oafish louts remember Mum,
And sleepless children's hearts are glad,
    And Christmas-morning bells say 'Come!'
Even to shining ones who dwell
Safe in the Dorchester Hotel.

And is it true? And is it true,
    This most tremendous tale of all,
Seen in a stained-glass window's hue,
    A Baby in an ox's stall?
The Maker of the stars and sea
Become a Child on earth for me?

And is it true? For if it is,
    No loving fingers tying strings
Around those tissued fripperies,
    The sweet and silly Christmas things,
Bath salts and inexpensive scent
And hideous tie so kindly meant,

No love that in a family dwells,
    No carolling in frosty air,
Nor all the steeple-shaking bells
    Can with this single Truth compare—
That God was Man in Palestine
And lives today in Bread and Wine.

LONDON

When I returned from school I found we'd moved:
'53 Church Street. Yes, the slummy end'—
A little laugh accompanied the joke,
For we were Chelsea now and we had friends
Whose friends had friends who knew Augustus John:
We liked bold colour schemes—orange and black—
And clever daring plays about divorce
At the St. Martin's. Oh, our lives were changed!
Ladies with pearls and hyphenated names
Supplanted simpler aunts from Muswell Hill:
A brand-new car and brand-new chauffeur came
To carry off my father to the Works.
                Old Hannah Wallis left:
For years she'd listened to me reading verse;

Tons, if you added them, of buttered toast
Had she and I consumed through all the days
In happy Highgate. Now her dear old face,
Black bonnet, sniffs and comfortable self
Were gone to Tottenham where her daughter lived.
    What is it first breeds insecurity?
Perhaps a change of house? I missed the climb
By garden walls and fences where a stick,
Dragged on the palings, clattered to my steps.
I missed the smell of trodden leaves and grass,
Millfield and Merton Lanes and sheep-worn tracks
Under the hawthorns west of Highgate ponds.
I missed the trams, the few North London trains,
The frequent Underground to Kentish Town.
Here in a district only served by bus,
Here on an urban level by the Thames—
I never really liked the Chelsea house.
'It's simply sweet, Bess,' visitors exclaimed,
Depositing their wraps and settling down
To a nice rubber. 'So artistic, too.'
To me the house was poky, dark and cramped,
Haunted by quarrels and the ground-floor ghost.
I'd slam behind me our green garden door—
Well do I recollect that bounding thrill!—
And hare to Cheyne Gardens—free! free! free!—
By Lawrence Street and Upper Cheyne Row,
Safe to the tall red house of Ronnie Wright.
    Great was my joy with London at my feet—
All London mine, five shillings in my hand
And not expected back till after tea!
Great was our joy, Ronald Hughes Wright's and mine,
To travel by the Underground all day
Between the rush hours, so that very soon
There was no station, north to Finsbury Park,
To Barking eastwards, Clapham Common south,
No temporary platform in the west
Among the Actons and the Ealings, where
We had not once alighted. Metroland
Beckoned us out to lanes in beechy Bucks—
Goldschmidt and Howland (in a wooden hut
Beside the station): 'Most attractive sites
Ripe for development'; Charrington's for coal;
And not far off the neo-Tudor shops.
We knew the different railways by their smells.
The City and South reeked like a changing-room;

13

Its orange engines and old rolling-stock,
Its narrow platforms, undulating tracks,
Seemed even then historic. Next in age,
The Central London, with its cut-glass shades
On draughty stations, had an ozone smell—
Not seaweed-scented ozone from the sea
But something chemical from Birmingham.
When, in a pause between the stations, quiet
Descended on the carriage we would talk
Loud gibberish in angry argument,
Pretending to be foreign.
                                        Then I found
Second-hand bookshops in the Essex Road,
Stacked high with powdery leather flaked and dry,
Gilt letters on red labels—Mason's *Works*
(But volume II is missing), Young's *Night Thoughts*,
Falconer's *Shipwreck* and *The Grave* by Blair,
A row of Scott, for certain incomplete,
And always somewhere Barber's *Isle of Wight*;
The antiquarian works that no one reads—
Church Bells of Nottingham, *Baptismal Fonts*
('Scarce, 2s. 6d., a few plates slightly foxed').
Once on a stall in Farringdon Road I found
An atlas folio of great lithographs,
Views of Ionian Isles, flyleaf inscribed
By Edward Lear—and bought it for a bob.
Perhaps one day I'll find a 'first' of Keats,
Wedged between Goldsmith and *The Law of Torts*;
Perhaps—but that was not the reason why
Untidy bookshops gave me such delight.
It was the smell of books, the plates in them,
Tooled leather, marbled paper, gilded edge,
The armorial book-plate of some country squire,
From whose tall library windows spread his park
On which this polished spine may once have looked,
From whose twin candlesticks may once have shone
Soft beams upon the spacious title-page.
Forgotten poets, parsons with a taste
For picturesque descriptions of a hill
Or ruin in the parish, pleased me much;
But steel engravings pleased me most of all—
Volumes of London views or Liverpool,
Or Edinburgh, 'The Athens of the North'.
I read the prose descriptions, gazed and gazed
Deep in the plates, and heard again the roll

Of market-carts on cobbles, coach-doors slammed
Outside the posting inn; with couples walked
Toward the pillared entrance of the church
'Lately erected from designs by Smirke';
And sauntered in some newly planted square.
Outside the bookshop, treasure in my hands,
I scarcely saw the trams or heard the bus
Or noticed modern London: I was back
With George the Fourth, post-horns, street-cries and bells.
'More books,' my mother sighed as I returned;
My father, handing to me half-a-crown,
Said, 'If you must buy books, then buy the best.'
   All silvery on frosty Sunday nights
Were City steeples white against the stars.
And narrowly the chasms wound between
Italianate counting-houses, Roman banks,
To this church and to that. Huge office-doors,
Their granite thresholds worn by weekday feet
(Now far away in slippered ease at Penge),
Stood locked. St. Botolph this, St. Mary that
Alone stood out resplendent in the dark.
I used to stand by intersecting lanes
Among the silent offices, and wait,
Choosing which bell to follow: not a peal,
For that meant somewhere active; not St. Paul's,
For that was too well-known. I liked things dim—
Some lazy Rector living in Bexhill
Who most unwillingly on Sunday came
To take the statutory services.
A single bell would tinkle down a lane;
My echoing steps would track the source of sound—
A cassocked verger, bell-rope in his hands,
Called me to high box pews, to cedar wood
(Like incense where no incense ever burned),
To ticking gallery-clock, and charity bench,
And free seats for the poor, and altar-piece—
Gilded Commandment boards—and sword-rests made
For long-discarded aldermanic pomp.
A hidden organist sent reedy notes
To flute around the plasterwork. I stood,
And from the sea of pews a single head
With cherries nodding on a black straw hat
Rose in a neighbouring pew. The caretaker?
Or the sole resident parishioner?
And so once more, as for three hundred years,

This carven wood, these grey memorial'd walls
Heard once again the Book of Common Prayer,
While somewhere at the back the verger, now
Turned Parish Clerk, would rumble out 'Amen.'
'Twas not, I think, a conscious search for God
That brought me to these dim forgotten fanes.
Largely it was a longing for the past,
With a slight sense of something unfulfilled;
And yet another feeling drew me there,
A sense of guilt increasing with the years—
'When I am dead you will be sorry, John'—
Here I could pray my mother would not die.
Thus were my London Sundays incomplete
If unaccompanied by Evening Prayer.
How trivial used to seem the Underground,
How worldly looked the over-lighted west,
How different and smug and wise I felt
When from the east I made my journey home!

Charles Causley

I wrote my first poems while I was in the Royal Navy. Up till 1940, I had scarcely left the small town in Cornwall where I was born. What affected me as much as anything during those wartime years was the fact that the companion who left with me for the Navy on that same day was later drowned in a convoy to northern Russia. From that moment, I found myself haunted by the words in the twenty-fourth chapter of St Matthew: 'Then shall two be in the field; the one shall be taken, and the other left'.

So it was that the earliest poems arose directly from wartime experience. Some were elegies for lost comrades; others were studies of the disasters and humours that war strews round with terrible and obvious prodigality. Another was a portrait of a Chief Petty Officer in which the central figure, by turns comic and sinister, becomes finally one of pathos: a barnacle-encrusted relic of a man who was once the eager young seaman of the battle of Jutland in 1916. The opening of the poem echoes, deliberately, the opening of the poem by Walter Pater (1839–94) on the Mona Lisa.

> She is older than the rocks among which she sits;
> Like the Vampire,
> She has been dead many times,
> And learned the secrets of the grave;
> And has been a diver in deep seas,
> And keeps their fallen day about her.

As well as the inevitable wartime subjects of separation, love, death in far and lonely places, I have also been obsessed by the theme of lost innocence. 'Nursery Rhyme of Innocence and Experience' is a picture of a particular series of events. It is also concerned with the mysteries of growing up—emotionally and imaginatively, as well as physically—into a world in which what is most hoped for often arrives too late, or when it is least wanted.

My first contact with the physical world of a poet was when, as a small child, I was shown the house at Teignmouth where John Keats, in 1818, had nursed his dying younger brother. I remembered how the river Teign was stained the colour of blood by the red soil of Devon. Three years later, the poet himself had died in Rome. So the nightingale in 'Keats at Teignmouth' is a reference not only to the 'Ode to a Nightingale', but also to Keats himself as a marvellously-tongued maker of poetry. There is something of this feeling, too, in 'At Grantchester', which partly concerns another young poet —Rupert Brooke, buried at Skyros in 1915—with God alone knows how much poetry then unwritten: poetry that may have differed in form and nature from anything he had produced before.

I say that this poem partly concerns Brooke because I do not think it can be emphasised enough that a poem may be all things to all people. It exists on many levels of meaning. We should beware of trying to nail down too precisely just what we imagine a poem to be 'about'. It should touch us at many points of our lives; and, like human life itself, it may constantly reveal new and hitherto unguessed-at aspects of its nature.

Similarly, in 'Innocent's Song', the surface of the poem constantly changes, rather in the manner of a film 'dissolve'; and lurking behind its lines is the threat of the all-destroying bomb. We remember the Massacre of the Innocents, coming so swiftly after the birth of Christ. The poem, then, is 'about'—among other things—the meaning of meaning, and the importance of questioning and testing what is presented to us as unassailable truth. A ballad like 'Charlotte Dymond' is not so much an account of a murder, as a question-mark poised above the killer and the killed, with the key to the poem contained in the words,

> Ask which of these two lovers
> The most deserves your prayers.

What a poem 'means' is something that the writer as well as the reader each must decide alone. Only one thing is certain: that, unlike arithmetic, the correct answers may all be right, yet all be different.

KING'S COLLEGE CHAPEL

When to the music of Byrd or Tallis,
    The ruffed boys singing in the blackened stalls,
The candles lighting the small bones on their faces,
    The Tudors stiff in marble on the walls,

There comes to evensong Elizabeth or Henry,
    Rich with brocade, pearl, golden lilies, at the altar,
The scarlet lions leaping on their bosoms,
    Pale royal hands fingering the crackling psalter,

Henry is thinking of his lute and of backgammon,
    Elizabeth follows the waving song, the mystery,
Proud in her red wig and green jewelled favours;
    They sit in their white lawn sleeves, as cool as history.

THE SEASONS IN NORTH CORNWALL

O spring has set off her green fuses
    Down by the Tamar today,
And careless, like tidemarks, the hedges
    Are bursting with almond and may.

Here lie I, waiting for old summer,
    A red face and straw-coloured hair has he:
I shall meet him on the road from Marazion
    And the Mediterranean Sea.

September has flung a spray of rooks
    On the sea-chart of the sky,
The tall shipmasts crack in the forest
    And the banners of autumn fly.

My room is a bright glass cabin,
    All Cornwall thunders at my door,
And the white ships of winter lie
    In the sea-roads of the moor.

KEATS AT TEIGNMOUTH

Spring 1818

By the wild sea-wall I wandered
  Blinded by the salting sun,
While the sulky Channel thundered
  Like an old Trafalgar gun.

And I watched the gaudy river
  Under trees of lemon-green,
Coiling like a scarlet bugle
  Through the valley of the Teign.

When spring fired her fusilladoes
  Salt-spray, sea-spray on the sill,
When the budding scarf of April
  Ravelled on the Devon hill,

Then I saw the crystal poet
  Leaning on the old sea-rail;
In his breast lay death, the lover,
  In his head, the nightingale.

INNOCENT'S SONG

Who's that knocking on the window,
Who's that standing at the door,
What are all those presents
Lying on the kitchen floor?

Who is the smiling stranger
With hair as white as gin,
What is he doing with the children
And who could have let him in?

Why has he rubies on his fingers,
A cold, cold crown on his head,
Why, when he caws his carol,
Does the salty snow run red?

Why does he ferry my fireside
As a spider on a thread,
His fingers made of fuses
And his tongue of gingerbread?

Why does the world before him
Melt in a million suns,
Why do his yellow, yearning eyes
Burn like saffron buns?

Watch where he comes walking
Out of the Christmas flame,
Dancing, double-talking:

Herod is his name.

AT GRANTCHESTER

Bank Holiday. A sky of guns. The river
Slopping black silver on the level stair.
A war-memorial that aims for ever
Its stopped, stone barrel on the enormous air.

A hoisted church, its cone of silence stilling
The conversations of the crow, the kite.
A coasting chimney-stack, advancing, filling
With smoking blossom the lean orchard light.

The verse, I am assured, has long ceased ticking
Though the immortal clock strikes ten to three,
The fencing wasp fights for its usual picking
And tongues of honey hang from every tree.

The swilling sea with its unvarying thunder
Searches the secret face of famous stone.
On the thrown wind blown words like hurt birds wander
That from the maimed, the murdered mouth have flown.

FOR AN EX-FAR EAST PRISONER OF WAR

I am that man with helmet made of thorn
Who wandered naked in the desert place,
Wept, with the sweating sky, that I was born
And wore disaster in my winter face.

I am that man who asked no hate, nor pity.
I am that man, five-wounded, on the tree.
I am that man, walking his native city,
Hears his dead comrade cry, *Remember me!*

I am that man whose brow with blood was wet,
Returned, as Lazarus, from the dead to live.
I am that man, long-counselled to forget,
Facing a fearful victory, to forgive:

And seizing these two words, with the sharp sun
Beat them, like sword and ploughshare, into one.

SONG OF THE DYING GUNNER A.A.1

Oh mother my mouth is full of stars
As cartridges in the tray
My blood is a twin-branched scarlet tree
And it runs all runs away.

Oh *Cooks to the Galley* is sounded off
And the lads are down in the mess
But I lie done by the forrard gun
With a bullet in my breast.

Don't send me a parcel at Christmas time
Of socks and nutty and wine
And don't depend on a long weekend
By the Great Western Railway line.

Farewell, Aggie Weston, the Barracks at Guz,
Hang my tiddley suit on the door
I'm sewn up neat in a canvas sheet
And I shan't be home no more.

H.M.S. *Glory*

Notes. 'Aggie Weston's' is the familiar term used by sailors to describe the
hostels founded in many seaports by Dame Agnes Weston. 'Guz' is naval
slang for Devonport.

CHIEF PETTY OFFICER

He is older than the naval side of British history,
And sits
More permanent than the spider in the enormous wall.
His barefoot, coal-burning soul,
Expands, puffs like a toad, in the convict air
Of the Royal Naval Barracks at Devonport.

Here, in depôt, is his stone Nirvana:
More real than the opium-pipes,
The uninteresting relics of his Edwardian foreign-commission.
And, from his thick stone box,
He surveys with a prehistoric eye the hostilities-only ratings.

He has the face of the dinosaur
That sometimes stares from old Victorian naval photographs:
That of some elderly lieutenant
With boots and a celluloid Crippen-collar,
Brass buttons and cruel ambitious eyes of almond.

He was probably made a Freemason in Hong Kong.
He has a son (on War Work) in the Dockyard,
And an appalling daughter
In the W.R.N.S.
He writes on your draft-chit,
Tobacco-permit or request-form
In a huge antique Borstal hand,
And pins notices on the board in the Chiefs' Mess
Requesting his messmates not to
Lay on the billiard-table.
He is an anti-Semite, and has somewhat reactionary views,
And reads the pictures in the daily news.

And when you return from the nervous Pacific
Where the seas
Shift like sheets of plate-glass in the dazzling morning;
Or when you return
Browner than Alexander, from Malta,
Where you have leaned over the side, in harbour,
And seen in the clear water
The salmon-tins, wrecks and tiny explosions of crystal fish,
A whole war later
He will still be sitting under a pusser's clock
Waiting for tot-time,
His narrow forehead ruffled by the Jutland wind.

Notes. 'Hostilities-only ratings' were those in the Royal Navy for the duration
of the war. Anything described as 'pusser's' is naval property, as issued by
the 'Pusser' or Paymaster.

CONVOY

Draw the blanket of ocean
Over the frozen face.
He lies, his eyes quarried by glittering fish,
Staring through the green freezing sea-glass
At the Northern Lights.

He is now a child in the land of Christmas:
Watching, amazed, the white tumbling bears
And the diving seal.
The iron wind clangs round the icecaps,
The five-pointed dogstar
Burns over the silent sea,

And the three ships
Come sailing in.

AT THE BRITISH WAR CEMETERY, BAYEUX

I walked where in their talking graves
And shirts of earth five thousand lay,
When history with ten feasts of fire
Had eaten the red air away.

I am Christ's boy, I cried, I bear
In iron hands the bread, the fishes.
I hang with honey and with rose
This tidy wreck of all your wishes.

On your geometry of sleep
The chestnut and the fir-tree fly,
And lavender and marguerite
Forge with their flowers an English sky.

Turn now towards the belling town
Your jigsaws of impossible bone,
And rising read your rank of snow
Accurate as death upon the stone.

About your easy heads my prayers
I said with syllables of clay.
What gift, I asked, shall I bring now
Before I weep and walk away?

Take, they replied, the oak and laurel.
Take our fortune of tears and live
Like a spendthrift lover. All we ask
Is the one gift you cannot give.

DEATH OF AN AIRCRAFT

An incident of the Cretan campaign, 1941
To George Psychoundakis

One day on our village in the month of July
An aeroplane sank from the sea of the sky,
   White as a whale it smashed on the shore
   Bleeding oil and petrol all over the floor.

The Germans advanced in the vertical heat
To save the dead plane from the people of Crete,
   And round the glass wreck in a circus of snow
   Set seven mechanical sentries to go.

Seven stalking spiders about the sharp sun
Clicking like clockwork and each with a gun,
   But at *Come to the Cookhouse* they wheeled about
   And sat down to sausages and sauerkraut.

Down from the mountain burning so brown
Wriggled three heroes from Kastelo town,
   Deep in the sand they silently sank
   And each struck a match for a petrol-tank.

Up went the plane in a feather of fire
As the bubbling boys began to retire
   And, grey in the guardhouse, seven Berliners
   Lost their stripes as well as their dinners.

Down in the village, at murder-stations,
The Germans fell in friends and relations:
   But not a Kastelian snapped an eye
   As he spat in the air and prepared to die.

Not a Kastelian whispered a word
Dressed with the dust to be massacred,
   And squinted up at the sky with a frown
   As three bubbly boys came walking down.

One was sent to the county gaol
Too young for bullets if not for bail,
    But the other two were in prime condition
    To take on a load of ammunition.

In Archontiki they stood in the weather
Naked, hungry, chained together:
    Stark as the stones in the market-place,
    Under the eyes of the populace.

Their irons unlocked as their naked hearts
They faced the squad and their funeral-carts.
    The Captain cried, 'Before you're away
    Is there any last word you'd like to say?'

'I want no words,' said one, 'with my lead,
Only some water to cool my head.'
    'Water,' the other said, ' 's all very fine
    But I'll be taking a glass of wine.

'A glass of wine for the afternoon
With permission to sing a signature-tune!'
    And he ran the *raki* down his throat
    And took a deep breath for the leading note.

But before the squad could shoot or say
Like the impala he leapt away
    Over the rifles, under the biers,
    The bullets rattling round his ears.

'Run!' they cried to the boy of stone
Who now stood there in the street alone,
    But, 'Rather than bring revenge on your head
    It is better for me to die,' he said.

The soldiers turned their machine-guns round
And shot him down with a dreadful sound
    Scrubbed his face with perpetual dark
    And rubbed it out like a pencil mark.

But his comrade slept in the olive tree
And sailed by night on the gnawing sea,
    The soldier's silver shilling earned
    And, armed like an archangel, returned.

COWBOY SONG

I come from Salem County
  Where the silver melons grow,
Where the wheat is sweet as an angel's feet
  And the zithering zephyrs blow,
I walk the blue bone-orchard
  In the apple-blossom snow,
When the teasy bees take their honeyed ease
  And the marmalade moon hangs low.

My Maw sleeps prone on the prairie
  In a boulder eiderdown,
Where the pickled stars in their little jam-jars
  Hang in a hoop to town.
I haven't seen Paw since a Sunday
  In eighteen seventy-three
When he packed his snap in a bitty mess-trap
  And said he'd be home by tea.

Fled is my fancy sister
  All weeping like the willow,
And dead is the brother I loved like no other
  Who once did share my pillow.
I fly the florid water
  Where run the seven geese round,
O the townsfolk talk to see me walk
  Six inches off the ground.

Across the map of midnight
  I trawl the turning sky,
In my green glass the salt fleets pass
  The moon her fire-float by.
The girls go gay in the valley
  When the boys come down from the farm,
Don't run, my joy, from a poor cowboy,
  I won't do you no harm.

The bread of my twentieth birthday
  I buttered with the sun,
Though I sharpen my eyes with lovers' lies
  I'll never see twenty-one.
Light is my shirt with lilies,
  And lined with lead my hood,
On my face as I pass is a plate of brass,
  And my suit is made of wood.

MY FRIEND MALONEY

My friend Maloney, eighteen,
  Swears like a sentry,
Got into trouble two years back
  With the local gentry.

Parson and squire's sons
  Informed a copper.
The magistrate took one look at Maloney.
  Fixed him proper.

Talked of the crime of youth,
  The innocent victim.
Maloney never said a blind word
  To contradict him.

Maloney of Gun Street,
  Back of the Nuclear Mission,
Son of the town whore,
  Blamed television.

Justice, as usual, triumphed,
  Everyone felt fine.
Things went deader.
  Maloney went up the line.

Maloney learned one lesson:
  Never play the fool
With the products of especially a minor
  Public school.

Maloney lost a thing or two
  At that institution.
First shirt, second innocence,
  The old irresolution.

Found himself a girl-friend,
  Sharp suit, sharp collars.
Maloney on a moped,
  Pants full of dollars.

College boys on the corner
  In striped, strait blazers
Look at old Maloney,
  Eyes like razors.

You don't need talent, says Maloney.
  You don't need looks.
All I got you got, fellers.
  You can keep your thick books.

Parson got religion,
  Squire, in the end, the same.
The magistrate went over the wall.
  Life, said Maloney, 's a game.

Consider then the case of Maloney,
  College boys, parson, squire, beak.
Who was the victor and who was the victim?
  Speak.

NURSERY RHYME OF
INNOCENCE AND EXPERIENCE

I had a silver penny
  And an apricot tree
And I said to the sailor
  On the white quay

'Sailor O sailor
  Will you bring me
If I give you my penny
  And my apricot tree

'A fez from Algeria
  An Arab drum to beat
A little gilt sword
  And a parakeet?'

And he smiled and he kissed me
  As strong as death
And I saw his red tongue
  And I felt his sweet breath

*'You may keep your penny
  And your apricot tree
And I'll bring your presents
  Back from sea.'*

O the ship dipped down
   On the rim of the sky
And I waited while three
   Long summers went by

Then one steel morning
   On the white quay
I saw a grey ship
   Come in from sea

Slowly she came
   Across the bay
For her flashing rigging
   Was shot away

All round her wake
   The seabirds cried
And flew in and out
   Of the hole in her side

Slowly she came
   In the path of the sun
And I heard the sound
   Of a distant gun

And a stranger came running
   Up to me
From the deck of the ship
   And he said, said he

'*O are you the boy*
   Who would wait on the quay
With the silver penny
   And the apricot tree?

'*I've a plum-coloured fez*
   And a drum for thee
And a sword and a parakeet
   From over the sea.'

'O where is the sailor
   With bold red hair?
And what is that volley
   On the bright air?

'O where are the other
    Girls and boys?
And why have you brought me
    Children's toys?'

THE BALLAD OF CHARLOTTE DYMOND

*Charlotte Dymond, a domestic servant aged eighteen, was murdered
near Rowtor Ford on Bodmin Moor on Sunday, 14th April 1844, by her
young man, a crippled farm-hand, Matthew Weeks, aged twenty-two.
A stone marks the spot.*

It was a Sunday evening
    And in the April rain
That Charlotte went from our house
    And never came home again.

Her shawl of diamond redcloth,
    She wore a yellow gown,
She carried the green gauze handkerchief
    She bought in Bodmin town.

About her throat her necklace
    And in her purse her pay:
The four silver shillings
    She had at Lady Day.

In her purse four shillings
    And in her purse her pride
As she walked out one evening
    Her lover at her side.

Out beyond the marshes
    Where the cattle stand,
With her crippled lover
    Limping at her hand.

Charlotte walked with Matthew
    Through the Sunday mist,
Never saw the razor
    Waiting at his wrist.

Charlotte she was gentle
    But they found her in the flood
Her Sunday beads among the reeds
    Beaming with her blood.

Matthew, where is Charlotte,
    And wherefore has she flown?
For you walked out together
    And now are come alone.

Why do you not answer,
    Stand silent as a tree,
Your Sunday worsted stockings
    All muddied to the knee?

Why do you mend your breast-pleat
    With a rusty needle's thread
And fall with fears and silent tears
    Upon your single bed?

Why do you sit so sadly
    Your face the colour of clay
And with a green gauze handkerchief
    Wipe the sour sweat away?

Has she gone to Blisland
    To seek an easier place,
And is that why your eye won't dry
    And blinds your bleaching face?

'Take me home!' cried Charlotte,
    'I lie here in the pit!
A red rock rests upon my breasts
    And my naked neck is split!'

Her skin was soft as sable,
    Her eyes were wide as day,
Her hair was blacker than the bog
    That licked her life away.

Her cheeks were made of honey,
    Her throat was made of flame
Where all around the razor
    Had written its red name.

As Matthew turned at Plymouth
    About the tilting Hoe,
The cold and cunning Constable
    Up to him did go:

'I've come to take you, Matthew,
  Unto the Magistrate's door.
Come quiet now, you pretty poor boy,
  And you must know what for.'

'She is as pure,' cried Matthew,
  'As is the early dew,
Her only stain it is the pain
  That round her neck I drew!

'She is as guiltless as the day
  She sprang forth from her mother.
The only sin upon her skin
  Is that she loved another.'

They took him off to Bodmin,
  They pulled the prison bell,
They sent him smartly up to Heaven
  And dropped him down to Hell.

All through the granite kingdom
  And on its travelling airs
Ask which of these two lovers
  The most deserves your prayers.

And your steel heart search, Stranger,
  That you may pause and pray
For lovers who come not to bed
  Upon their wedding day,

But lie upon the moorland
  Where stands the sacred snow
Above the breathing river,
  And the salt sea-winds go.

Patric Dickinson

Author's Introduction

The only poem of his own any poet is wholly interested in is his next poem. There are very few poets who have all that they have written by heart, and could reproduce their poems from memory if all the texts were destroyed. Equally, there are very few poets who have no desire whatsoever to publish their poems. Once a poem is published it has to live its own life. What the poet meant to say has turned into what the poem itself unalterably does say. We are all—or should be—insatiably curious about each other. If you like a picture or a symphony or a building you want to know what the creator of it is like. What usually you mean is what he is like when he is not creating: what his life is—his love affairs, what he enjoys eating and drinking. But creators have dual lives which are never separate. Unlike people who do not create, they make themselves public, they publish, they share, they aim to communicate. It is not 'love that makes the world go round' but gossip—about love; about death; about all human affairs. You do not often hear gossip about sculptures or operas, but you do hear and read in popular newspapers about their creators. To bring this point to a head: almost nothing is known about Shakespeare, almost everything about Keats. How does this affect your feeling towards what they wrote? A poet's life *is* what he writes—and publishes. In general, poets publish not only 'for love of fame' but because they hope these poems can contribute to the sum of other people's lives. Some poets go beyond 'hope' and feel people 'ought' to read their poems.

I think that if you are compelled towards any work of art, either by the artist, or by society, or by education, the essence of communication is impaired. When people cease to communicate freely, they are apt to hit each other, as an argument. No art is a weapon or truly can be. Poetry uses words, the words we all use, so it is most vulnerable to abuses.

Harold Monro, himself a poet, once wrote gloomily that the only thing people really like to know about a poet is that he is dead. The false romance surrounding the deaths, say, of Shelley or Brooke or Dylan Thomas, is what he resents, for it diverts attention away from the poems they wrote. I could, whilst I am alive, annotate these poems of mine which have been so well chosen. Each of them has private circumstances. But if I had wanted to put footnotes I would have published them, as in one case I did.

Equally if I had to *describe* the style in which I write I think it would mean that it was imperceptible—as it well may be!

There is no 'school for studying' poetry as there are academies and conservatories. A poet needs must lifelong love and continue to read all the poetry he can; must practise his art in his own way, whatever the narrow dictates of fashion. What I write is the result of trying to find my own way to express what I can express no way else. On my way I continue to ask the help of *all* poets because our aim is poems—poems which will fulfil and enliven and enrich experience. I have spent most of my working life in the service of poetry one way or another. I have loved to do so. I know that 'there is pleasure there'. But the pleasures poetry offers are to be personally discovered. A poem communicates to every single reader individually. Critics use the word 'response' when considering a reader. This really does imply that poems pose questions. Often these are questions no one need answer; sometimes that no one *can* answer. But, truly, no poem is a full stop; or it is no poem.

JODRELL BANK

Who were they, what lonely men
Imposed on the fact of night
The fiction of constellations
And made commensurable
The distances between
Themselves, their loves, and their doubt
Of governments and nations?
Who made the dark stable

When the light was not? Now
We receive the blind codes
Of spaces beyond the span
Of our myths, and a long dead star
May only echo how
There are no loves nor gods
Men can invent to explain
How lonely all men are.

THE ONSET

The sun has set; the curtain stirs;
   The first outriders of the night
Have marked your window as they pass,
   And in the little room you wait
The onset of the universe.

Alone you watch the stars come out
   Like touchstones of the Ultimate
In an infinity of doubt—
   And still the mind insatiate
Seeks for a measure more remote.

The soul within you feigns asleep
   But murmurs like a midland shell
Sea-haunted by the primal deep;
   The body hears the passing-bell
Bury the day it craves to keep;

Listen, the drums of midnight beat,
    The dawn is here, the banners wave,
And you shall not admit defeat
    When others raise upon your grave
The white flag of a winding-sheet.

ON DOW CRAG

The shepherd on the fell,
With his wild expert cry
Like an atavistic owl,
His dog a vicarious eye

And obedient tentacle,
His rhythm and routine
So nearly animal,
Is yet completely man.

A buzzard rounds its noose
Of hunger high above,
Its eye can split a mouse
If but a whisker move.

—So will it live and die;
No gene within the shell
Shall change its timeless eye
On the shepherd, on the fell,

On the boy who sets the foot
Of the future on Dow Crag,
Who assumes the shepherd's lot,
The buzzard in its egg,

Whose view is incomplete
Till he sees small and far
Like a toy at his feet,
Down on the western shore,

The beautiful cooling-towers
Of Calder Hall as strange
As Zimbabwe, as the powers
Of man to suffer change.

BLUEBELLS

Like smoke held down by frost
The bluebells wreathe in the wood.
Spring like a swan there
Feeds on a cold flood:

But the winter woodmen know
How to make flame
From sodden December faggots,
They can make the blue smoke climb.

Picked flowers wilt at once,
They flare but where they are;
The swan will not sing nor the fire thrive
In a town-watered jar:

But the winter woodmen know
The essential secret burning;
The fire at the earth's core
In touch with the turning sun.

THE SCALE OF THINGS

I was holding my son's hand
As he pattered the low wall.
He could break a leg, I knew,
So dangerous the fall
In the lilliput two year old
World he was moving in—
This marsh and river scene
Where everything named to him
Is paradise-new, it is not
The brutal world we mean
By 1951.

The full fed emerald green
Pedestrian caterpillar
Seeking its place of trance
To lie in till its wings
In that amazing change
Give it a new range
In the dark honeyed air. . . .
What chance brought it there
Under the poised foot?

There was the scale of things
That no handhold of love
Could keep them from.
I was the wretched Greek
Who from a scene as slight
Divined the furious doom
That dogs humanity,
And knowing he was right
Still went to bed that night
In hopes of dreamless sleep.
But lay awake. As I.

THE REDWING

The winter clenched its fist
And knuckles numb with frost
Struck blind at the blinding snow.
It was hard for domestic creatures,
Cows, humans, and such, to get
Shelter and warmth and food.
And then the redwings came,
Birds of the open field,
The wood, the wild, only
Extremity makes them yield.

I must admit that never
Before that day when thaw
Bled red to white in the west
Had I seen a redwing, but there
Where ivy-berries offered
A last everlasting lost
Hope of life I held
A redwing in my hand,
Still warm, and was it dead?
It had toppled from a tree
Too weak too frail to fill
Its crop before the frost
Again asked for the cost
Of a winter dosshouse rest.
So I saw what it was like.

Never before had I seen
A redwing, now a hundred

Hopped through the shivering town
Unrecognised, unknown
To most who saw them save
Simply as 'birds'. They came
As poets come among us,
Driven in from the wild
Not asking nor expecting
To be recognised for what
They are—if they are not
The usual thrush you can
Identify them dead.

I held it in my hand,
I knew that it was dead,
But still I willed it to live
Not asking nor expecting
Many to understand
Why I must will it so.
But I know what a redwing is,
And I know how I know.

THE DAM

This was our valley, yes,
Our valley till they came
And chose to build the dam.
All the village worked on it
And we were lucky of course
All through the slump we had
Good jobs; they were too well paid
For the water rose ninety feet,

And covered our houses; yes—
In a midsummer drought
The old church-spire pokes out
And the weather cock treads the wind
But we were lucky of course
We were—most of us—laid on
Like the water, to the town.
Somehow, I stayed behind.

I work on the dam, yes—
Do you think the drowned ash-trees

Still have faint impulses
When Spring's up here I wonder?
I was lucky of course
But oh there's a lot of me
Feels like a stifled tree
That went on living, under.

They turn on their taps, yes,
In the dusty city and drink:
Now is it that we sink
Or that the waters rise?
They are lucky of course
But as they go to work
There's an underwater look
In their street-shuttered eyes.

This was our valley, yes,
And I live on the dam
And in my sight the dream
Still drowns the dreamer's home
But I am lucky of course
For in a time of drought
Within me and without
I see where I came from.

COMMON TERNS

Quiet as conscience on the Stock Exchange
I crept across a gradient of shelving shingle
To where in a gravel-working water lay
Brackish and thick with weed, slate-blue and viscous.

Out on a spit were common terns in hundreds:
Terns with their delicate staggered swallow-wings
And striding lilting flight and hovering flutter
Like kestrels into the wind, and sheer stoop
Straight for the darting goby in the pool.

And as I rose above the shingle crest
They burst into the air like an explosion,
A white gusher, a quarter-mile-high fountain
Mushrooming out into fragments, yet each perfect,
A column of shrieking milling sound-at-pressure,
Terribly like man's work—as if they were
An atomic bomb and I some engineer.

I felt my human agony then to the full,
That I for simile of that natural vision
Should so conclusively immediately choose
Utter destruction absolute desolation;
And sat there numb and grievous, ashamed to move,
As wildly they whirled and wheeled and slowly settled,
Bright sediment down the blue glass of air.

THE ROYAL MILITARY CANAL

Hythe to the River Rother

I

In agony of mind, in the west country,
Safe in a beautiful green solitude,
Coleridge sweated imagining invasion.*

That is where they will land
Said the General imagining invasion—
In Dymchurch Bay, Rye Bay, all along there.
This is what you must do.

I must write a poem. I must make them feel
Somehow the horror, the wounds, the bloody shambles,
I must break this inhuman indifference to suffering.

What must we do?

You must cut a defensive canal
From Hythe to the River Rother:
It is no use telling me that it cannot be done.

Where are the words, where are the spades?
Hundreds of sweating men, week after week;
This is where they will land.

What am I to say?

Report the canal is finished,
The north bank built as a rampart,
The length some fifteen miles.

Where are the words?

* *Fears in Solitude* (1807).

43

A pity, that invasion came to nothing.
We were never able to test the canal in action.
Better plant trees on the north bank to bind it.

II

One hundred and forty years of falling leaves,
From the first thin autumn each year recruiting number,
Weeping, falling, brief and expendible,
And we indifferent to them as to soldiers,
Layer upon layer into the soft canal,
And the trunks swelling with slow Victorian Empire.

III

Come here; do you see the notice?
This is officially beautiful, to be preserved
By the National Trust. The Royal Military Canal.
Cut out of terror and urgency, a defensive measure,
Hurriedly hundreds of sweating men for weeks—
And now it is beautiful. Yes, truly it is so.
Along the grass-covered rampart blackberries grow
Under the elms, and Marbled White butterflies
In their short season flicker over the blossoms
Casting their eggs on the wing—a strange miracle
To ponder, as Coleridge would have, now as we walk
    along
Gathering flowering reeds with their lush muddy smell.

IV

Some of the trees are dead.
Like huge cast antlers, gray and inert and naked,
They pray dead prayers to the contemporary sun,
Under whose light we move in living terror.
They will all die soon.

V

Sit here; under this old dead tree—
This is where they will land.
There is nothing to stop them but the narrow canal,
So beautiful this evening in old age.

44

Will, in a hundred years, our fearful preparations
Anywhere in the world be beautiful
And innocent, a natural solitude
In which to plant our fears?—(if they might grow
New trees along these banks!)—
                            Tonight I fear
More for the flowering reeds, the Marbled Whites,
And the Kingfisher we expect each minute,
Than for ourselves.
I fear for all Nature under the threat of Man,
Running the dustbowl through his nickel fingers—
Even in direst fear not planting even the grain
That will bind his children's flesh
To their soft pliant bones.

I feel more lost beside this old canal,
More desperate for man's indifference
Than ever Coleridge. And what is there to do?

Where are the words? Where are the spades?
This is where they will land.

THE ROMAN WALL

The cars speed up and down. Under the surface lie
Foundations of the Wall, like the fossil vertebrae
Of an extinct animal. The cars speed up and down,
Their radios lilt and lull, till from his blind watch-tower
A reader gives them news, half-heeded and half-heard
Between Wallsend and Carlisle, of contending worlds to choose,
Of the molten core of Power on whose thin crust they ride.
Above and Roman-straight is a bomber's vapour-trail,
Below at the gate of Cilurnum the Emperor's post from Rome.

Here the Astures watched shivering in the rain,
Conquered auxiliaries, cavalrymen from Spain,
But eating and drinking from mass-produced Samian-ware,
Pretending to like baths, and generally behaving
In a low Roman fashion, defending a civilisation
Few would enjoy by saving and few understand;
Yet trained to fight to the death for their fostermotherland
As if they could really care for the system of its Law—
And now the Emperor's word: the order to withdraw.

In their ruined bath-house I try to re-animate the scene,
To hear the steamy shouts of the glistening naked men,
Till the last man is out, and dressed in his time again;
The stoker draws the fires, the water soon goes cold.
Naked to silence here by the long-broken bounds
Of the Pax Romana I shiver and watch the sky.
Where they laid their uniforms in lockers of neat stone
Long folded echoes lie, but I dare not put them on
Lest they clothe me with a voice: *Suppose our language die?*

The cars speed up and down the temporal surfaces,
The vapour-trail has turned to innocent-looking cloud;
Between Wallsend and Carlisle there is no news today.
The lulling music drowns the order to withdraw,
Half-heeded and half-heard, it drowns the living word
That condemns the innocent by process of natural Law.
Yesterday they went with underhopes of home
And mostly glad to go—how impotent to save
A Rome already burned perhaps their leaders know.

HEARTBREAK HOUSE

Shaw's Corner to let, unfurnished

Your Irish wit made you bequeath
This hideous dump to English dust?—
Even in life we viewed you with
A national mistrust.

LINES FOR AN EMINENT POET AND CRITIC

He has come to such a pitch
Of self-consciousness that he
Dare not scratch, if he has the itch,
For fear he is the flea.

GEOLOGIC

This fossil in my hand,
When first it was understood,
Unmade the sea, the land,
Undated God,

And man was forced to look
Into his heart alone,
Divining, as it broke,
An older stone.

LAMENT FOR THE GREAT YACHTS

For Tom Rice Henn

Suddenly into my dream why should they come
Closehauled from the west, from Cowes, beating
Out to the Nab with bones in their delicate teeth,
    The old-fashioned beautiful cutters
        The great yachts,
            Bowsprit and topsail, gaff and flying jib:
            Shamrock glittering green;
            Candida, Astra, Lulworth, white; and *Britannia*
Ebony-black and bronze as she heels hard
When the old King takes the wheel and brings her up
Another two points to the wind and the sea hisses
        And her lee goes flowing under.

And carving the water, saving her time, the *Westward*,
The noblest ever, the perfect racing schooner;
Why should they suddenly steer from the bright blue
    Of a boyhood summer out on the popping seaweed
        And barnacle rocks—
            My naked feet slow-savouring their teeth
            And my gray shorts wet to the thighs—
            I saw them there and loved their ravishing grace
With a siren's lust, I wanted them to be mine
And I wanted the King to win, always to win
As he did when the wind blew hard and the Ryde steamers
        Were queasy even in Portsmouth with towny trippers.

And I hated the *Lulworth*, she was the ugliest:
And once as the great yachts passed Fort Gilkicker
Out at Spithead, there passed them hurrying inward
    The *Mauretania* the truly most beautiful
        Of steamships ever built—
            Perfection fabulous, never again to be known,
            Never never again,
            And I saw these thoroughbred creatures of seaman-kind
        Race on the English-summer-coloured-water

47

Again in a dream, yet human eye shall see them
To the world's end never never again
    In the stiff sou'wester bucking and lively as light.

O and in fact I remember them: thousands must.
But we shall die, and few as lucky as I
Will have a bright dream couple with memory
   In sudden and unpremeditable love—
      May my luck hold!
        For men may explain the logic and dialectic
        That dragged them to the bottom
        To let the silt and slimy water-dust
   Settle upon their pride of wood and metal,
But racing I saw them, darlings of the weather,
Identities of skill, anatomies perfect,
      And now for ever lost for ever lost.

And I have felt their white sails crumple and fall
And the bare masts seem too tall, the hulls riding
Sadly like sleeping bodies, until my spirit
   Blew gale-force and dragged my anchored body
      In never mournful mood,
        But in a joyful agony of acceptance:
        As waking I accept the twenty years
        That have moved the furniture of my own flesh
   From that small room upon a rocky pier
Where I looked out to see my holiday
And wanted it to keep, to keep for ever
      Under my pillow like a beloved toy.

And there it lay, to bring after twenty years
An absolute joy, a strange and marvellous thing:
How little it is I can pass on or share!
   They had their Royal week of Cowes Regatta,
      Fireworks and flags
        And ships like jewellers cutting the precious sea.
        But my words are neither Solent winds nor tides,
        They are things forgotten, sentimental chimes,
Bowsprit and topsail, gaff and flying jib.
Their meanings wash against this later day
Rubbing the names off: *Astra, Candida,*
     Shamrock, Westward, Lulworth, Britannia.

Clifford Dyment

I am an autobiographical poet—using that word in a broad sense. I don't take subjects from literature, legend, or history and make poems out of them, but write about my own experiences—what I see, what I do, what happens to me, what I remember, what I feel and think. In other words, I write poems of self-exploration. I don't do this out of arrogance or vanity, or because I disapprove of poems on abstract themes, but because I am an undogmatic person and feel I have the right to speak only for myself.

Because I write out of my own experience my poems vary as my experience varies. No person is always the same person. On Monday morning we might have a sour approach to life and curse the street band for playing such corny music, but on Friday evening we might well feel in love with the whole world and drop half a crown into the begging hat; a remark that in one mood we regard as a sneer, in another we accept as a compliment; our reaction to a given situation varies with our physical state; and as we grow older we change our enthusiasms, affections, opinions, habits. In my own case I have had political and religious phases; I have had periods of conformity and of rebellion; I have been serious and frivolous; and there have been times when I wanted to write in an orthodox manner and others when I felt a need to experiment. I have always tried to write sincerely as I felt at the time and have never forced myself to maintain a particular style or a particular type of poem or to be consistent with an immediately recognisable image of myself or to write in accordance with the outlook of a school, region, or decade. 'To thine own self be true' might be my motto as a poet—though I know that it makes my work difficult to classify. At various times I have been described as a nature poet, a religious poet, a war poet, a poet of machinery; as classical and romantic; as an exponent of the plain style and as a poet rich in imagery; as narrow and wide in range; as lucid and obscure; as traditional and *avant-garde*; and I have been compared with William Blake, Robert Burns, John Clare, A. E.

Housman, Gerard Manley Hopkins, the composer Dvorak, and the painter L. S. Lowry. But why must I—or any poet—be labelled? There is far too much labelling today: commuters, consumers, company directors; teenagers, tourists, trade unionists—but don't we come in all shapes, sizes, and colours of mind and personality?

The two points I have made about my work—that it's written from personal experience and shows the diversity of personal experience—are exemplified in the poems included in this book. 'Holidays in Childhood' and 'The Carpenter' are memories, recalling the village in South Wales where I spent the first years of my life and where my father was the carpenter. 'Fox', 'A Switch Cut in April', and 'The Swans' might be called nature poems, but I think they aren't merely that: the imagery is drawn from the countryside, though the real subject in each case is something else: in 'Fox' it is defeat, in 'A Switch Cut in April' it is elation, in 'The Swans' (which records an incident I witnessed on the Grand Union Canal) it is violence. By contrast, 'The Winter Trees', 'Coming of the Fog', 'The Dark City', and 'Bahnhofstrasse' are urban poems: 'The Winter Trees' points to the hardship of individualism and the ease of conformity, 'Coming of the Fog' says something good about smog, 'The Dark City' suggests the powerful emotional appeal of a lighted window at night, and 'Bahnhofstrasse' (the name of the principal shopping street in Zürich) is an impression of the glittering luxury of a prosperous city's 'West End' as dusk falls. The largest group of my poems in this anthology is one of indirectly religious poems: ' "From Many a Mangled Truth a War is Won" ' is concerned with the humility we must accept as a result of what theologians call the doctrine of original sin—we must strive in an imperfect world to use imperfect means to gain imperfect ends; 'Carrion' and 'Man and Beast' ask questions about love and hate, sin and guilt; 'The Axe in the Wood' is, in its deeper meaning, an anti-war poem—it has taken centuries to grow this tree, it has taken generations to grow one casualty; 'The King of the Wood' is an affirmation of life even though—in the words of the prayer book—we know that 'in the midst of life we are in death'—or, to put it another way, 'Le roi est mort, vive le roi!'; ' "Savage the Daylight and Annihilate Night" ' is a despairing protest against the idiocy which leads men to work so industriously for self-destruction. 'The Desert' and 'The Raven' are my most recent poems and originated in dreams; the imagery and the symbolism are derived from the unconscious but the meaning of the poems is clear I think: 'The Desert' is a vision of two survivors lamenting the world devastated by atomic warfare and 'The Raven' deplores man's hostility to what he doesn't understand.

I have heard different interpretations of the last two poems, but this doesn't worry me because I don't think that a poem has necessarily its author's definitive meaning and no other. A poem is rather like Lord Kitchener's finger in the famous World War I poster: during its composition it points at the poet, but afterwards it points at everyone who reads it. Different readers see different things in a poem according to their experiences and temperaments. To give a simple instance: suppose a poet uses 'bread' as an image—this will vary in significance for (a) a maker of old-fashioned crusty loaves whose livelihood is threatened by a take-over bid from a big plant bakery; (b) a girl who is slimming; and (c) a mal-nourished child in an under-developed country. One might almost say that a poem has as many meanings as it has readers, so that if some interpretations of my poems differ from my own I shan't be surprised or perturbed.

THE CARPENTER

With a jack plane in his hands
My father the carpenter
Massaged the wafering wood,
Making it white and true.

He was skilful with his saws,
Handsaw, bowsaw, hacksaw,
And ripsaw with fishes' teeth
That chewed a plank in a second.

He was fond of silver bits,
The twist and countersink—
And the auger in its pit
Chucking shavings over its shoulder.

I remember my father's hands,
For they were supple and strong
With fingers that were lovers—
Sensuous strokers of wood:

He fondled the oak, the strong-man
Who holds above his head
A record-breaking lift
Of thick commingled boughs;

And he touched with his finger tips
Dark boards of elm and alder,
Spruce, and cherry for lathes
That turned all days to spring.

My father's hands were tender
Upon my tender head,
But they were massive on massive
Beam for building a house,

And delicate on the box wood
Leaning against the wall
As though placed there in a corner
For a moment and then forgotten,

And expert as they decoded
Archives unlocked by the axe—
The pretty medullary rays
Once jammed with a traffic of food

To a watched and desired tree
That he marked and felled in the winter,
The tracks of tractors smashing
The ground where violets grew,

Then bound in chains and dragged
To the slaughtering circular saw:
A railway dulcimer
Rang the passing bell

Of my father's loved ones,
Though there was no grief in him
Caressing the slim wood, hearing
A robin's piccolo song.

HOLIDAYS IN CHILDHOOD

Last year Harold was making a boat
For his small cousin from the north country.
His tools and timber were not very good,
But he had clever fingers, the youth Harold,
And he had shaped the hull with all his skill,
Given it narrow lines to slip through water,
And cut the keel to give a seabird's poise.
The hull was finished, mast and bowsprit fitted,
Waiting for halyards, blocks, sails fore and aft
To change the shaven wood into a yacht.
It was going to be a trim and speedy ship.

The hull is in the outhouse now,
With the thick knife beside it.
It still looks like a swift and sturdy vessel,
And its prow seems eager for the waves.
The mountain still looms distantly beyond the town,
With the sky above it, and the strong winds
Whistling in the grasses as they always whistle.
The shops and houses are all just the same,
And the trams rattle by as they did last year—
Though this year Harold is dead.

FOX

Exploiter of the shadows
He moved among the fences,
A strip of action coiling
Around his farmyard fancies.

With shouting, fields are shaken;
The spinneys give no shelter:
There is delight for riders,
For hounds a tooth in shoulder.

The creature tense with wildness
Knows death is sudden falling
From fury into weary
Surrendering of feeling.

A SWITCH CUT IN APRIL

This thin elastic stick was plucked
From gradual growing in a hedge,
Where early mist awakened leaf,
And late slow hands with spiral stroke
Smoothed slumber from the weighted day,
While flowers drooped with colours furled.

I cut quick circles with the stick:
It whistles in the April air
An eager song, a bugle call,
A signal for the running feet,
For rising flyer flashing sun,
And windy tree with surging crest.

This pliant wood like expert whip
Snaps action in its voice, commands
A quiver from the sloth, achieves
A jerk in buds; with stinging lash
A spring of movement in the stiff
And sleeping limbs of winter land.

Stick plucked and peeled, companions lost,
Torn from its rooted stock: I hold
Elate and lithe within my hands

Winged answer to the wings' impulse,
The calyx breaking into flame,
The crystal cast into the light.

THE SWANS

Midstream they met. Challenger and champion,
They fought a war for honour
Fierce, sharp, but with no honour:
Each had a simple aim and sought it quickly.
The combat over the victor sailed away
Broken, but placid as is the gift of swans,
Leaving his rival to his shame alone.
I listened for a song, according to story,
But this swan's death was out of character—
No giving up of the grace of life
In a sad lingering music.
I saw the beaten swan rise on the water
As though to outreach pain, its webbed feet
Banging the river helplessly, its wings
Loose in a last hysteria. Then the neck
Was floating like a rope and the swan was dead.
It drifted away and all around it swan's-down
Bobbed on the river like children's little boats.

THE WINTER TREES

Against the evening sky the trees are black,
Iron themselves against the iron rails;
The hurrying crowds seek cinemas or homes,
A cosy hour where warmth will mock the wind.
They do not look at trees now summer's gone,
For fallen with their leaves are those glad days
Of sand and sea and ships, of swallows, lambs,
Of cricket teams, and walking long in woods.

Standing among the trees a shadow bends
And picks a cigarette-end from the ground;
It lifts the collar of an overcoat,
And blows upon its hands and stamps its feet—
For this is winter, chastiser of the free,
This is the winter, kind only to the bound.

COMING OF THE FOG

Only the lamps are live
To tell of the town's quiet death.
Trees loom at intervals
Looped in their lonely veils,
In alien law aloof.

Glad to be free of the street's strictness,
Idling enrapt as a child from school,
I range in the mind:
I flock with starlings and become a gong
Trembling with the call of continents;
And now I am a shepherd in the night
Who sees his field a heaven and is afraid—

A welcome mist, coming gently as seraph,
With infinite key throwing open the bars
That monitor what the heart would try:
I reach my hand to my brother in Asia,
And speak my love like the gay skylark.

THE DARK CITY

The lighted city is dark, but somewhere a bus
Glows and flares up in a hearth of coal-black space
And with its headlights singles out a face
Lost in a night of enormous loneliness.

Lost in the night of enormous loneliness
Which is his life, man looks for signs of light:
They are the small camp fires which put to flight
The beasts that prowl towards his helplessness.

The beasts that prowl towards our helplessness
Are brave in darkness, but in light they run
To deep subconscious caves in the mind of man
For whom a light is a home in homelessness.

BAHNHOFSTRASSE

Night slides down the mountain side
In an avalanche unheard, the dust
Rolling into the streets of Zürich

As mist moth-soft towards the lights:
It wraps up brooches of glass in gauzes,
Clocks are diamond pendants worn
By a wealth of space, women are flattering
Soft focus portraits, the flashing
Foyers of cafés are enormous carnivals
Of orchids and roses, the air is furry
Lined against snow and solitude.

'FROM MANY A MANGLED TRUTH A WAR IS WON'

From many a mangled truth a war is won
   And who am I to oppose
   War and the lie and the pose
Asserting a lie is good if a war be won?

From many a mangled truth a war is won
   And many a truth has died
   That has lived undenied
For always there must be loss that a war be won.

From many a mangled truth a war is won
   And when no thought is pure
   Who of us can be sure
Of lie and truth and war when the war is won?

THE AXE IN THE WOOD

I stopped to watch a man strike at the trunk
Of a tree grown strong through many centuries.
His quick axe, sharp and glittering, struck deep,
And yellow chips went spinning in the air—
And I remember how I liked the sight
Of poise and rhythm as the bright axe swung.
A man who fells a tree makes people watch,
For glory seems to crowd upon the axe.

I know the answers to the chance reproach:
How old the tree was, and how dangerous,
How it might fall, how timber in a stack
Had more good in it than a growing tree—
But I saw death cut down a thousand men
In that tall lovely legacy of wood.

CARRION

A yellowhammer in her mouth, the cat came mewing
To me. It was such a bird as I had seen
Skim the hedge like a ball of the sun
Hurled by a starchild gaming in the wheat.

That was in summer. Now it is autumn,
I burning the leaves of a brave year dead
And gazing at the yellowhammer the cat abandoned,
Shrunken, soaked, but with a bright plume yet.

I stir the body: it is a shell stuffed with maggots.
They uncurl, startled by this threat to life—
And I, with human—so far holy!—love,
Hate maggots and cat, and long for golden wings.

MAN AND BEAST

Hugging the ground by the lilac tree,
With shadows in conspiracy,

The black cat from the house next door
Waits with death in each bared claw

For the tender unwary bird
That all the summer I have heard

In the orchard singing. I hate
The cat that is its savage fate,

And choose a stone with which to send
Slayer, not victim, to its end.

I look to where the black cat lies,
But drop my stone, seeing its eyes—

Who is it sins now, those eyes say,
You the hunter, or I the prey?

THE KING OF THE WOOD

Winter: winter in the woods
Is the bone that was the beauty,
The bough that lives the leaf:
The food supplies sink low
And the hedgehog and badger know the hour is late.

Comes snow—the scouting flakes
Nipping out of the north
Followed by bulky brigades
Falling with formidable lust
On land where evil and warm the weevil sleeps.

Spring: the leaves of the chestnut
Hang in the branches like bats;
Bluebells flood into valleys
Where butterflies dry wet wings
And the cock bird lords it in song on his terrain.

This is the season of primrose,
Woodruff, and anemone—
And the season of caterpillars
Of the mottled umber moth
Fattening ambition in a thousand worlds of plenty.

Summer: welcome the woods
When the air sweats in the sun!
Here is a draught of shade
In a cellar deep and dark
Where barrels are so tall they sway like trees.

Now ants are on the hunt
Each for a swag of syrup—
And the felted beech coccus
Seeks out the straight young tree
To lay the foundation stone of a leaning tower.

Autumn: the sky more blue
Than any flower or crystal;
The yellow and wrinkled face
Of the wood is streaked with wounds
As the catkins of the birches slide to the soil.

Burgled boxes with ermine
Lining drop their conkers
Among loot of acorns for squirrels—
And into the earth descends
The cockchafer beetle's larva to mine a future.

'SAVAGE THE DAYLIGHT AND ANNIHILATE NIGHT'

Savage the daylight and annihilate night
Anger in me that rises to destroy
Not evil only, which is a common thing,
But good also: such public shame is sweet.
Yes, sweet I say in defiance of the saints
Timorously peeping from the safe house
Of religious platitude and political honour:
Sweet is the violence without compassion,
Heroic the hand that chokes the holy flame.

Oh, man is huge over the little world,
Darkening it with pride. The darkness falls
Unfailingly and forever, and all this folly
Of grandeur so surely fatal angers me
Till I call to the heavens for the redeeming shock
Of a rage that ravishes even the angels.

THE DESERT

Beside a dune high as a tree
    But spreading no tree's shade
A man and boy sat silently
    Working at their trade.

A heap of bones lay on the sand
    Like barkless staves of wood;
And near it lay a second heap
    Polished with thickening blood.

One bone, two bones, three bones were
    Chosen by the man
Who made of them a heart's shape, wide
    As his two hands would span.

The man and boy sat hour by hour
    Calmly, coolly, dumb,
Feeling the scarlet heat as though
    Their blackened skins were numb.

A third heap soon rose at their side
    Like boughs laid for a pyre:
The boy's hand went to it and took
    From many lyres one lyre.

It was a lyre in shape, but where
    The stream of music springs
The lyre was nought, a mouth crying
    Wordlessly for strings.

The boy reached to the heap that shone
    Untouched on the sand
And from its bloody muteness took
    A bloody speaking hand.

He fixed the voice in place, then more,
    And soon the lyre was strung—
A frame made of three human bones,
    Each string a human tongue.

The old man took the brilliant lyre
    And struck its cords of red;
The boy rapt by his side stood up
    As a snake rears up its head

And with no smile and with no sigh
    Moved to the lyre's sounds
In a world all dust save for a man,
    A dancer, and three mounds.

THE RAVEN

    A raven crouched in a tree.
    It lived in the sky like me.

    I stared at the night in the tree:
    I felt its eye warm me.

What shock was shaking the tree?
Why was there blood on me?

From the world into the tree
Stones sprang and hissed round me.

They were killing the bird in the tree,
The raven that cheered me.

I hurried out of my tree—
The people greeted me:

They saw no bird in the tree.
They were very friendly to me.

Ted Hughes

Introduction

Ted Hughes's first book of poems, *The Hawk in the Rain*, was published in 1957. Many of the poems are notable for what has been called a 'verbal belligerence'. This violence of expression is occasioned by his view of the natural world with its noise and cruelty. Ted Hughes has said that 'what excites my imagination is the war between vitality and death'. Many of his poems are concerned with animals, their vigour and ruthlessness. Even in sleep the hawk rehearses 'perfect kills'—

> I kill where I please because it is all mine.
> There is no sophistry in my body:
> My manners are tearing off heads—

The tomcat 'will take the head clean off your simple pullet, is unkillable'; pike are 'killers from the egg', and thrushes are terrifying —'nothing but bounce and stab and a ravening second'.

Violence extends to the world of men in 'Bayonet Charge' and to the weather in such poems as 'November', with its drilling rain. In 'Six Young Men' and 'Griefs for Dead Soldiers' Ted Hughes writes of the violence and heroism of the First World War. There are three griefs for men killed in action, and the writer, to quote Mr A. E. Dyson, 'explores each in isolation. The "secretest" grief, which is that of the widow, is one thing:

> Closer than thinking
> The dead man hangs around her neck, but never
> Close enough to be touched, or thanked even,
> For being all that remains in a world smashed. . . .

the "truest" grief, which is that of the calm craftsman digging graves for the unburied dead as they wait "like brides to surrender their limbs" is another. But apart from these, unmodified by them, and "mightiest", is the public grief at the cenotaph. Here, the deaths are ideally celebrated. The dead become symbols, as enduring as the marble of the cenotaph itself; pure heroism, protected from the irony which the other two more human griefs would undoubtedly generate if allowed to mix, is celebrated as enduring magnificence

> their souls
> Scrolled and supporting the sky, and the national sorrow,
> Over the crowds that know of no other wound,
> Permanent stupendous victory.

'In almost any other post-World-War-II poet one can think of, these lines could scarcely be anything other than ironic; and the "griefs" of the widow, and of the agents of oblivion, would be among the stuff of irony. Ted Hughes alone manages to isolate the heroic—not denying the other facts, but denying their power to negate the quality of heroism itself. Perhaps it is no surprise that he should write of the First rather than the Second World War, and be obsessed by such types of warfare (bayonet charges, trench fighting) as belong to the pre-hydrogen age, when personal heroism was still of merit in the scheme of things. The quality of violence he writes of, however, is sufficiently up-to-date; one cannot write off his achievement as mere nostalgia for the good old days of meaningful slaughter.

'The major theme in the poems is power; and power thought of not morally, or in time, but absolutely—in a present which is often violent and self-destructive, but isolated from motive or consequence, and so unmodified by the irony which time confers. For Ted Hughes power and violence go together: his own dark gods are makers of the tiger, not the lamb. He is fascinated by violence of all kinds, in love and in hatred, in the jungle and the arena, in battle, murder and sudden death. Violence, for him, is the occasion not for reflection, but for *being*; it is a guarantee of energy, of life, and most so, paradoxically, when it knows itself in moments of captivity, pain or death. He looks at the caged jaguar, as it hurries "enraged Through prison darkness after the drills of its eyes", and finds victory in its untamed will—

> there's no cage to him
> More than to the visionary his cell.
> His stride is wildernesses of freedom.'

BAYONET CHARGE

Suddenly he awoke and was running—raw
In raw-seamed hot khaki, his sweat heavy,
Stumbling across a field of clods towards a green hedge
That dazzled with rifle fire, hearing
Bullets smacking the belly out of the air—
He lugged a rifle numb as a smashed arm;
The patriotic tear that had brimmed in his eye
Sweating like molten iron from the centre of his chest—

In bewilderment then he almost stopped—
In what cold clockwork of the stars and the nations
Was he the hand pointing that second? He was running
Like a man who has jumped up in the dark and runs
Listening between his footfalls for the reason
Of his still running, and his foot hung like
Statuary in mid-stride. Then the shot-slashed furrows

Threw up a yellow hare that rolled like a flame
And crawled in a threshing circle, its mouth wide
Open silent, its eyes standing out.
He plunged past with his bayonet towards the green hedge.
King, honour, human dignity, etcetera
Dropped like luxuries in a yelling alarm
To get out of that blue crackling air
His terror's touchy dynamite.

GRIEFS FOR DEAD SOLDIERS

I

Mightiest, like some universal cataclysm,
Will be the unveiling of their cenotaph:
The crowds will stand struck, like the painting of a terror
Where the approaching planet, a half-day off,
Hangs huge above the thin skulls of the silenced birds;
Each move, each sound, a fresh-cut epitaph—
Monstrousness of the moment making the air stone.

Though thinly, the bugle will then cry,
The dead drum tap, and the feet of the columns
And the sergeant-major's voice blown about by the wind
Make these dead magnificent, their souls
Scrolled and supporting the sky, and the national sorrow,
Over the crowds that know of no other wound,
Permanent stupendous victory.

II

Secretest, tiniest, there, where the widow watches on the table
The telegram opening of its own accord
Inescapably and more terribly than any bomb
That dives to the cellar and lifts the house. The bared
Words shear the hawsers of love that now lash
Back in darkness, blinding and severing. To a world
Lonely as her skull and little as her heart

The doors and windows open like great gates to a hell.
Still she will carry cups from table to sink.
She cannot build her sorrow into a monument
And walk away from it. Closer than thinking
The dead man hangs around her neck, but never
Close enough to be touched, or thanked even,
For being all that remains in a world smashed.

III

Truest, and only just, here, where since
The battle passed the grass has sprung up
Surprisingly in the valleyful of dead men.
Under the blue sky heavy crow and black fly move.
Flowers bloom prettily to the edge of the mass grave
Where spades hack, and the diggers grunt and sweat.
Among the flowers the dead wait like brides

To surrender their limbs; thud of another body flung
Down, the jolted shape of a face, earth into the mouth—
Moment that could annihilate a watcher!
Cursing the sun that makes their work long
Or the black lively flies that bite their wrists,
The burial party works with a craftsman calm.
Weighing their grief by the ounce, and burying it.

SIX YOUNG MEN

The celluloid of a photograph holds them well—
Six young men, familiar to their friends.
Four decades that have faded and ochre-tinged
This photograph have not wrinkled the faces or the hands.
Though their cocked hats are not now fashionable,
Their shoes shine. One imparts an intimate smile,
One chews a grass, one lowers his eyes, bashful,
One is ridiculous with cocky pride—
Six months after this picture they were all dead.

All are trimmed for a Sunday jaunt. I know
That bilberried bank, that thick tree, that black wall,
Which are there yet and not changed. From where these sit
You hear the water of seven streams fall
To the roarer in the bottom, and through all
The leafy valley a rumouring of air go.
Pictured here, their expressions listen yet,
And still that valley has not changed its sound
Though their faces are four decades under the ground.

This one was shot in an attack and lay
Calling in the wire, then this one, his best friend,
Went out to bring him in and was shot too;
And this one, the very moment he was warned
From potting at tin-cans in no-man's-land,
Fell back dead with his rifle-sights shot away.
The rest, nobody knows what they came to,
But come to the worst they must have done, and held it
Closer than their hope; all were killed.

Here see a man's photograph,
The locket of a smile, turned overnight
Into the hospital of his mangled last
Agony and hours; see bundled in it
His mightier-than-a-man dead bulk and weight:
And on this one place which keeps him alive
(In his Sunday best) see fall war's worst
Thinkable flash and rending, onto his smile
Forty years rotting into soil.

That man's not more alive whom you confront
And shake by the hand, see hale, hear speak loud,
Than any of these six celluloid smiles are,

Nor prehistoric or fabulous beast more dead;
No thought so vivid as their smoking blood:
To regard this photograph might well dement,
Such contradictory permanent horrors here
Smile from the single exposure and shoulder out
One's own body from its instant and heat.

ROARERS IN A RING

Snow fell as for Wenceslas.
   The moor foamed like a white
Running sea. A starved fox
   Stared at the inn light.

In the red gridded glare of peat,
   Faces sweating like hams,
Farmers roared their Christmas Eve
   Out of the low beams.

Good company kept a laugh in the air
   As if they tossed a ball
To top the skip of a devil that
   Struck at it with his tail,

Or struck at the man who held it long.
   They so tossed laughter up
You would have thought that if they did not
   Laugh, they must weep.

Therefore the ale went round and round.
   Their mouths flung wide
The cataract of a laugh, lest
   Silence drink blood.

And their eyes were screwed so tight,
   While their grand bellies shook—
O their flesh would drop to dust
   At the first sober look.

The air was new as a razor,
   The moor looked like the moon,
When they all went roaring homewards
   An hour before dawn.

Those living images of their deaths
    Better than with skill
Blindly and rowdily balanced
    Gently took their fall

While the world under their footsoles
    Went whirling still
Gay and forever, in the bottomless black
    Silence through which it fell.

DICK STRAIGHTUP

Past eighty, but never in eighty years—
Eighty winters on the windy ridge
Of England—has he buttoned his shirt or his jacket.
He sits in the bar-room seat he has been
Polishing with his backside sixty-odd years
Where nobody else sits. White is his head,
But his cheek high, hale as when he emptied
Every Saturday the twelve-pint tankard at a tilt,
Swallowed the whole serving of thirty eggs,
And banged the big bass drum for Heptonstall—
With a hundred other great works, still talked of.
Age has stiffened him, but not dazed or bent,
The blue eye has come clear of time:
At a single pint, now, his memory sips slowly,
His belly strong as a tree bole.

He survives among hills, nourished by stone and height.
The dust of Achilles and Cuchulain
Itches in the palms of scholars; thin clerks exercise
In their bed-sitters at midnight, and the meat salesman can
Loft fully four hundred pounds. But this one,
With no more application than sitting,
And drinking, and singing, fell in the sleet, late,
Dammed the pouring gutter; and slept there; and, throughout
A night searched by shouts and lamps, froze,
Grew to the road with welts of ice. He was chipped out at dawn
Warm as a pie and snoring.

The gossip of men younger by forty years—
Loud in his company since he no longer says much—
Empties, refills and empties their glasses.

Or their strenuous silence places the dominoes
(That are old as the house) into patterns
Gone with the game; the darts that glint to the dartboard
Pin no remarkable instant. The young men sitting
Taste their beer as by imitation,
Borrow their words as by impertinence
Because he sits there so full of legend and life
Quiet as a man alone.

He lives with sixty and seventy years ago,
And of everything he knows three quarters is in the grave,
Or tumbled down, or vanished. To be understood
His words must tug up the bottom-most stones of this village,
This clutter of blackstone gulleys, peeping curtains,
And a graveyard bigger and deeper than the village
That sways in the tide of wind and rain some fifty
Miles off the Irish sea.
                          The lamp above the pub-door
Wept yellow when he went out and the street
Of spinning darkness roared like a machine
As the wind applied itself. His upright walk,
His strong back, I commemorate now,
And his white blown head going out between a sky and an earth
That were bundled into placeless blackness, the one
Company of his mind.

Obit.

Now, you are strong as the earth you have entered.

This is a birthplace picture. Green into blue
The hills run deep and limpid. The weasel's
Berry-eyed red lock-head, gripping the dream
That holds good, goes lost in the heaved calm

Of the earth you have entered.

THE JAGUAR

The apes yawn and adore their fleas in the sun.
The parrots shriek as if they were on fire, or strut
Like cheap tarts to attract the stroller with the nut.
Fatigued with indolence, tiger and lion

Lie still as the sun. The boa-constrictor's coil
Is a fossil. Cage after cage seems empty, or
Stinks of sleepers from the breathing straw.
It might be painted on a nursery wall.

But who runs like the rest past these arrives
At a cage where the crowd stands, stares, mesmerised,
As a child at a dream, at a jaguar hurrying enraged
Through prison darkness after the drills of his eyes

On a short fierce fuse. Not in boredom—
The eye satisfied to be blind in fire,
By the bang of blood in the brain deaf the ear—
He spins from the bars, but there's no cage to him

More than to the visionary his cell:
His stride is wildernesses of freedom:
The world rolls under the long thrust of his heel.
Over the cage floor the horizons come.

THE HORSES

I climbed through woods in the hour-before-dawn dark.
Evil air, a frost-making stillness,

Not a leaf, not a bird,—
A world cast in frost. I came out above the wood

Where my breath left tortuous statues in the iron light.
But the valleys were draining the darkness

Till the moorline—blackening dregs of the brightening grey—
Halved the sky ahead. And I saw the horses:

Huge in the dense grey—ten together—
Megalith-still. They breathed, making no move,

With draped manes and tilted hind-hooves,
Making no sound.

I passed: not one snorted or jerked its head.
Grey silent fragments

Of a grey silent world.

I listened in emptiness on the moor-ridge.
The curlew's tear turned its edge on the silence.

Slowly detail leafed from the darkness. Then the sun
Orange, red, red erupted

Silently, and splitting to its core tore and flung cloud
Shook the gulf open, showed blue,

And the big planets hanging—.
I turned

Stumbling in the fever of a dream, down towards
The dark woods, from the kindling tops,

And came to the horses.
                              There, still they stood,
But now steaming and glistening under the flow of light,

Their draped stone manes, their tilted hind-hooves
Stirring under a thaw while all around them

The frost showed its fires. But still they made no sound.
Not one snorted or stamped,

Their hung heads patient as the horizons,
High over valleys, in the red levelling rays—

In din of the crowded streets, going among the years, the faces,
May I still meet my memory in so lonely a place

Between the streams and the red clouds, hearing curlews,
Hearing the horizons endure.

HAWK ROOSTING

I sit in the top of the wood, my eyes closed.
Inaction, no falsifying dream
Between my hooked head and hooked feet:
Or in a sleep rehearse perfect kills and eat.

The convenience of the high trees!
The air's buoyancy and the sun's ray
Are of advantage to me;
And the earth's face upward for my inspection.

My feet are locked upon the rough bark.
It took the whole of Creation
To produce my foot, my each feather:
Now I hold Creation in my foot

Or fly up, and revolve it all slowly—
I kill where I please because it is all mine.
There is no sophistry in my body:
My manners are tearing off heads—

The allotment of death.
For the one path of my flight is direct
Through the bones of the living.
No arguments assert my right:

The sun is behind me.
Nothing has changed since I began.
My eye has permitted no change.
I am going to keep things like this.

THRUSHES

Terrifying are the attent sleek thrushes on the lawn,
More coiled steel than living—a poised
Dark deadly eye, those delicate legs
Triggered to stirrings beyond sense—with a start,
                                        a bounce, a stab
Overtake the instant and drag out some writhing thing.
No indolent procrastinations and no yawning stares,
No sighs or head-scratchings. Nothing but bounce
                                        and stab
And a ravening second.

Is it their single-mind-sized skulls, or a trained
Body, or genius, or a nestful of brats
Gives their days this bullet and automatic
Purpose? Mozart's brain had it, and the shark's mouth
That hungers down the blood-smell even to a leak
                                        of its own
Side and devouring of itself: efficiency which
Strikes too streamlined for any doubt to pluck at it
Or obstruction deflect.

With a man it is otherwise. Heroisms on horseback,
Outstripping his desk-diary at a broad desk,
Carving at a tiny ivory ornament
For years: his act worships itself—while for him,

Though he bends to be blent in the prayer, how loud
                                                    and above what
Furious spaces of fire do the distracting devils
Orgy and hosannah, under what wilderness
Of black silent waters weep.

PIKE

Pike, three inches long, perfect
Pike in all parts green tigering the gold.
Killers from the egg: the malevolent aged grin.
They dance on the surface among the flies.

Or move, stunned by their own grandeur,
Over a bed of emerald, silhouette
Of submarine delicacy and horror.
A hundred feet long in their world.

In ponds, under the heat-struck lily pads—
Gloom of their stillness:
Logged on last year's black leaves, watching
                                               upwards.
Or hung in an amber cavern of weeds

The jaws' hooked clamp and fangs
Not to be changed at this date;
A life subdued to its instrument;
The gills kneading quietly, and the pectorals.

Three we kept behind glass,
Jungled in weed: three inches, four,
And four and a half: fed fry to them—
Suddenly there were two. Finally one

With a sag belly and the grin it was born with.
And indeed they spare nobody.
Two, six pounds each, over two feet long,
High and dry and dead in the willow-herb—

One jammed past its gills down the other's gullet:
The outside eye stared: as a vice locks—
The same iron in this eye
Though its film shrank in death.

A pond I fished, fifty yards across,
Whose lilies and muscular tench
Had outlasted every visible stone
Of the monastery that planted them—

Stilled legendary depth:
It was as deep as England. It held
Pike too immense to stir, so immense and old
That past nightfall I dared not cast

But silently cast and fished
With the hair frozen on my head
For what might move, for what eye might move.
The still splashes on the dark pond,

Owls hushing the floating woods
Frail on my ear against the dream
Darkness beneath night's darkness had freed,
That rose slowly towards me, watching.

VIEW OF A PIG

The pig lay on a barrow dead.
It weighed, they said, as much as three men.
Its eyes closed, pink white eyelashes.
Its trotters stuck straight out.

Such weight and thick pink bulk
Set in death seemed not just dead.
It was less than lifeless, further off.
It was like a sack of wheat.

I thumped it without feeling remorse.
One feels guilty insulting the dead,
Walking on graves. But this pig
Did not seem able to accuse.

It was too dead. Just so much
A poundage of lard and pork.
Its last dignity had entirely gone.
It was not a figure of fun.

Too dead now to pity.
To remember its life, din, stronghold
Of earthly pleasure as it had been,
Seemed a false effort, and off the point.

Too deadly factual. Its weight
Oppressed me—how could it be moved?
And the trouble of cutting it up!
The gash in its throat was shocking, but
                                    not pathetic.

Once I ran at a fair in the noise
To catch a greased piglet
That was faster and nimbler than a cat,
Its squeal was the rending of metal.

Pigs must have hot blood, they feel like ovens.
Their bite is worse than a horse's—
They chop a half-moon clean out.
They eat cinders, dead cats.

Distinctions and admirations such
As this one was long finished with.
I stared at it a long time. They were going
                                    to scald it,
Scald it and scour it like a doorstep.

ESTHER'S TOMCAT

Daylong this tomcat lies stretched flat
As an old rough mat, no mouth and no eyes.
Continual wars and wives are what
Have tattered his ears and battered his head.

Like a bundle of old rope and iron
Sleeps till blue dusk. Then reappear
His eyes, green as ringstones: he yawns wide red,
Fangs fine as a lady's needle and bright.

A tomcat sprang at a mounted knight,
Locked round his neck like a trap of hooks
While the knight rode fighting its clawing and bite.
After hundreds of years the stain's there

On the stone where he fell, dead of the tom
That was at Barnborough. The tomcat still
Grallochs odd dogs on the quiet,
Will take the head clean off your simple pullet,

Is unkillable. From the dog's fury,
From gunshot fired point-blank he brings
His skin whole, and whole
From owlish moons of bekittenings

Among ashcans. He leaps and lightly
Walks upon sleep, his mind on the moon.
Nightly over the round world of men,
Over the roofs go his eyes and outcry.

NOVEMBER

The month of the drowned dog. After long rain the land
Was sodden as the bed of an ancient lake,
Treed with iron and birdless. In the sunk lane
The ditch—a seep silent all summer—

Made brown foam with a big voice: that, and my boots
On the lane's scrubbed stones, in the gulleyed leaves,
Against the hill's hanging silence;
Mist silvering the droplets on the bare thorns

Slower than the change of daylight.
In a let of the ditch a tramp was bundled asleep:
Face tucked down into beard, drawn in
Under its hair like a hedgehog's. I took him for dead,

But his stillness separated from the death
Of the rotting grass and the ground. A wind chilled,
And a fresh comfort tightened through him,
Each hand stuffed deeper into the other sleeve.

His ankles, bound with sacking and hairy band,
Rubbed each other, resettling. The wind hardened;
A puff shook a glittering from the thorns,
And again the rains' dragging grey columns

Smudged the farms. In a moment
The fields were jumping and smoking; the thorns
Quivered, riddled with the glassy verticals.
I stayed on under the welding cold

Watching the tramp's face glisten and the drops on
                                                his coat
Flash and darken. I thought what strong trust
Slept in him—as the trickling furrows slept,
And the thorn-roots in their grip on darkness;

And the buried stones, taking the weight of winter;
The hill where the hare crouched with clenched teeth.
Rain plastered the land till it was shining
Like hammered lead, and I ran, and in the rushing wood

Shuttered by a black oak leaned.
The keeper's gibbet had owls and hawks
By the neck, weasels, a gang of cats, crows:
Some, stiff, weightless, twirled like dry bark bits

In the drilling rain. Some still had their shape,
Had their pride with it; hung, chins on chests,
Patient to outwait these worst days that beat
Their crowns bare and dripped from their feet.

SONG

O lady, when the tipped cup of the moon blessed you
You became soft fire with a cloud's grace;
The difficult stars swam for eyes in your face;
You stood, and your shadow was my place:
You turned, your shadow turned to ice,
          O my lady.

O lady, when the sea caressed you
You were a marble of foam, but dumb.
When will the stone open its tomb?
When will the waves give over their foam?
You will not die, nor come home,
          O my lady.

O lady, when the wind kissed you
You made him music for you were a shaped shell.
I follow the waters and the wind still
Since my heart heard it and all to pieces fell
Which your lovers stole, meaning ill,
       O my lady.

O lady, consider when I shall have lost you
The moon's full hands, scattering waste,
The sea's hands, dark from the world's breast,
The world's decay where the wind's hands have passed
And my head, worn out with love, at rest
In my hands, and my hands full of dust,
       O my lady.

James Kirkup

Author's Introduction

'The Submerged Village' was written after I had seen, in an illustrated magazine, a photograph of a reservoir formed in a Cumberland valley, where once there had been a village. At the time when the photograph was taken, there had been a long drought, and the level of the water had dropped so far that the steeple of the drowned village's church appeared above the surface. The thought of a submerged village had haunted me for a long time before that: I had always been fascinated by the idea of submarine cities and the oceanic life of the drowned. My first book of poems is called *The Drowned Sailor*, and my favourite Debussy prelude was 'La Cathédrale Engloutie', while his symphonic poem *La Mer* is one I listen to still with instinctive recognition of my element. The first twenty years of my life were spent in daily contact with the North Sea on the Durham and Northumberland coasts. During the Second World War, when my conscientious objection to war took me to many parts of England as a lumberjack and farm labourer, I visited the great inland lake of Semmerwater in the remote West Riding of Yorkshire several times (the first time in 1943) and was spellbound by the immensity, grandeur and loneliness of the place, and by the story of the village submerged beneath the water, from which the sound of a church bell was supposed to come at evening.

After the poem first appeared (in *The Listener*) many people wrote to me asking if I had written about submerged villages in districts as far apart as Cornwall, Wales, the Lake District, Scotland, the French Alps and Switzerland. My poem concerns a real place— though I no longer remember its name. It is no imaginary Lyonesse, but rather a sister to Goldsmith's 'The Deserted Village'. I have paid a kind of tribute to that great poem by using my 'containing' couplets at the end of each stanza. All is real in this poem, yet all is imaginary. There was no golden cross on the steeple in the photograph: I cannot remember, but it was probably a cock on a weathervane. But I wanted the cross, and so in my poem I put it there. The 'submerged' atmosphere was probably aided by memories of my visits to country churches that summer, with their windows greened and darkened by churchyard trees.

The connection between this poem and 'The Bowl of Goldfish', written one year later at Leeds, is fairly obvious.

'A City of the North' is Leeds, where I lived for two years (October 1950–October 1952). The 'sleek stone façades betraying honest brick behind' refers to the elaborate Queen Anne frontage of the Civic Hall and other notable public edifices.

There is little I can say about 'The Bowl of Goldfish' except that, like nearly all my poems, it is a joke to be seriously enjoyed. The form is influenced, very freely, by my admiration for La Fontaine and Gay. The 'watery element' here, as in so many of my 'water poems', was partly inspired by the 'Elegy on a Favourite Cat drowned in a Tub of Goldfish' and by George Darley's 'Nepenthe', 'Sea-Ritual' and 'The Mermaiden's Vesper-Hymn'. (My sea-poems also echo at times 'The Forsaken Merman'.)

'A Charm for the Ear-Ache' is set among a group of poems devoted to music. I wrote it in a Leeds winter when I was plagued by ear-ache. It cured me, and has cured others, of that distressing affliction.

'Ghosts, Fire, Water'. These panels were exhibited in London in 1956. I made several visits to see them, and was deeply impressed by their vision of war's horrors, worse than any Goya had ever known. At that time, I had no idea that I should ever go to live in Japan, but when I did reach that land, and visited Hiroshima in 1960, hoping to see the panels again, they were not on display. However, in 1963, at Nagasaki, I saw in the Peace Museum there yet another atom-bomb panel by these five artists. I cannot say anything about the poem. I hope it speaks for itself.

'No More Hiroshimas' should be read in conjunction with 'Ghosts, Fire, Water'. It, too, speaks for itself.

'To the Ancestral North' and 'For the 90th Birthday of Sibelius' go together. Both are, in quite different ways, expressions of my pride in a Viking ancestry and of my passion for loneliness, stillness, the sea. The work of Sibelius has always exerted a strange influence on my imagination, particularly the Violin Concerto, the First Symphony and the tone-poems *The Swan of Tuonela* and *The Return of Lemmenkainen.*

'To an Old Lady Asleep at a Poetry Reading' is based on an actual experience. Better than any of my poems it expresses my attitude towards poetry and towards human beings. I need hardly add that the poetry I was reading was not my own, but Dame Edith Sitwell's (*Still Falls the Rain*).

Raoul Ponchon is a not very well-known literary man of late nineteenth-century Paris. Though I am not a Christian, I like the personality of Christ and the story of his life.

V and VII from 'Seven Pictures from China'. This group of poems was inspired by a book of Chinese paintings that was given to me at Salamanca, Spain, where I wrote them in December 1958. They attempt to render the unique sense of perspective in Chinese land-scape painting—the sense of immense height and distance, the tinyness of man and his works in the vastnesses of mountains and plains.

'Sakunami' is the name of a hot-spring resort in the mountains of northern Japan, not far from the city of Sendai. The use of the word 'loudspeakers' in verse 1 should perhaps be explained. In many Japanese shopping-streets the shops have tape-recorded advertise-ments playing all the time through loudspeakers hung on lamp-posts outside. The word here is used as a verb. 'Straw-trussed trees': in winter, the Japanese cover their ornamental and dwarf trees with suits and caps of reeds or straw, to protect them from the cold. 'A red flag': every 'bus has a red flag which the conductor uses to guide the driver over difficult or dangerous country roads. 'The mats': these are finely-woven, pale-golden oblongs (when new, the sedge they are made of is pale-green) about 4 feet by 2 feet, which are stitched on wooden frames and laid together to form the floor of a Japanese room. The rice-wine (*saké*) is the national drink, and is usually drunk hot. 'Lemon chrysanthemum petals': these are from a special variety of edible chrysanthemum cultivated by the Japanese.

'Earthquake'. In actual fact, the kite was not there. I invented it, as I did the cross in 'The Submerged Village' to provide a suitable symbol—here the kite is a symbol of security and calm and philo-sophic indifference. Kite-flying is a popular male sport in certain districts of Japan, especially at the New Year. 'The metal gauze': the mosquito-screens over my windows of paper on sliding frames. The chest of drawers here is one of the specialties made in Sendai, and known as a *tansu*.

There is little to be said about 'Tea in a Space-Ship'. Like all poems, it is there to be enjoyed to the full, not talked about too much. There is an ironical reference to Rupert Brooke in line 3 of verse 4 (his 'Grantchester'). The poem is a rationalising of the irrational (the task of science today) in the polite terms of a British tea-party even madder than the Mad Hatter's.

'Rugby League Game' was inspired, like many of my poems, by an 'action photograph' from the back page of a newspaper. In it I try to express the fundamental absurdity of all sport, especially when played with deadly earnest. The contrast between the almost savage solemnity of the ritual of rugby football and the trite and trivial domesticity awaiting its heroes—pram-pushing on Sunday morning, for example, while wifey cooks the joint—is to me very funny. Why do they do it? What is the use of all that courage? (I loathe all organised games and never watch them or play them.) Courage is a very over-rated commodity, and I nearly always distrust it. It is something we should never be called upon to use, and it should never be invoked in the cause of 'just wars'. It often creates its own violence, as in rugby.

'A Visit to Brontëland'. The title was inspired by a joke I heard, when I was living in Leeds, from a dear old poet, Wilfrid Rowland Childe, who was also on the university staff. A literary lady belonging to the very culture-vulture Brontë Society was paying her first visit to the parsonage. She had lost her way at the bottom of the hill, and so she stopped a working man and said: 'Tell me, my good man, is this the way to Brontëland?' To which the man replied, politely: 'Ee, ah doan't know, missus, ah cum fra Haworth meself!'

In the poem I am particularly pleased by the use of two words—my own invention 'wuthered', whose source is obvious: and 'aspires', as in those days all the TV aerials were of an H shape. I like also the ambiguity in 'want' in the last line. This is a true, and not an artificial use of ambiguity. The first four verses are Betjemanesque—he is a poet I enjoy very much—but the last three are all my own. It is one of my favourite poems.

From SEVEN PICTURES FROM CHINA

v *Landscape, by Ch'êng Sui*

From a mountainside,
We look dizzily down
Through an ancient willow.

Across the bay
The peninsulas of rocks and trees
Fan the mist away
Into a poem on
A last inch of sky,
Indelible horizon.

In a narrow boat,
Curved and shallow as a leaf,
A lady and her boatman float
Upon the mist that hangs
Under and over their watery way.

She sits, with her white
Face lighting her black hair,
In the pale robe of ceremony.

The boatman in a pointed hat
Poles with dark hands
Their fragile craft
Towards a distant shore,
Where, set in a dry cliff among
Dark pines, a little house invents

A figure watching from an upper window
A dry leaf drifting on the misty bay.

VII *Autumn Grove After Rain, by Wen Tien*

Adrift in space,
The mountain's bare outline,
And a lower mountain's
Rocky waterfall—a white
Cleft on white mist—

With here a few
Slopes of pines,
And there a fall
Of mossy stones
That tumble soundlessly
Into a whiteness
That is either lake
Or sea or mist,
Or nothing—

On which a grove of trees
Floats away on flat rocks,
With a thatched summerhouse
And a tiny man
Fishing
From only
Half a bridge.

SAKUNAMI

In the city of Sendai, electric cold
Loudspeakers the crowded pavements
While snow stills the falling dusk
And shrouds the streets with freezing flags.

In the packed bus that sharply draws
The widening country round our eyes
The men are talking Saturday talk,
The girls smile with Sunday smiles.

In village gardens, snow
Caps all the straw-trussed trees;
The landscape's calligraphy unrolls
Its long winter picture's endless dreams.

Red-cheeked country children trot
And paddle in the turning snow:
Old women in dark clothes
Bear striped bundles down deep white lanes.

Wild workmen stamp their muffled clogs,
Blow tufts of steam into the churning air,
And in their bristling capes of reeds
Like porcupines plunge through a hedge of flakes.

At Shirasawa, the narrow bridges turn
To snowdrifts over rocky streams,
And the conductor goes with red flag
In the dramatic headlamps, to show the way.

Through the grey twilight, mountains
Hump their shaggy backs like camels.
The village shops are caves of fruit and toys;
On curved roofs, dark tiles are muffed with white.

Deep in the mountainous night
The lamps of Sakunami bleach the snow.
The mats in the sliding rooms are cool,
The pale rice-wine as warm as kisses.

The long bath grills us to the bone.
At Roman ease, up to the neck we lie
In hot spring-water from the boiling
Cauldrons of the earth, while candid snow,

A midwinter midnight's dream,
Flowers black boughs and green bamboos
With clumps of crystal, paper leaves
Beyond the ice-fringed windows of the bath.

In the cool-screened room the brazier glows:
Low lantern-light: soup steams: fresh oysters
Grey and silver in a white bowl
Of lemon chrysanthemum-petals.

We sleep on the floor in the house of wood
That creaks gently while the snow
Glides silently outside, like ghosts
Wandering houseless from suspended waterfalls of ice.

In the new morning at Sakunami
I sip a bowl of fragrant tea, feeling a quiet joy
As I watch from the floor of our tranquil room
The mountains soundlessly rising in the falling snow.

GHOSTS, FIRE, WATER

On the Hiroshima panels by Iri Maruki and Toshiko Akamatsu

These are the ghosts of the unwilling dead,
Grey ghosts of that imprinted flash of memory
Whose flaming and eternal instant haunts
The speechless dark with dread and anger.

Grey, out of pale nothingness their agony appears.
Like ash they are blown and blasted on the wind's
Vermilion breathlessness, like shapeless smoke
Their shapes are torn across the paper sky.

These scarred and ashen ghosts are quick
With pain's unutterable speech, their flame-cracked flesh
Writhes and is heavy as the worms, the bitter dirt;
Lonely as in death they bleed, naked as in birth.

They greet each other in a ghastly paradise,
These ghosts who cannot come with gifts and flowers.
Here they receive each other with disaster's common love,
Covering one another's pain with shrivelled hands.

They are not beautiful, yet beauty is in their truth.
There is no easy music in their silent screams,
No ordered dancing in their grief's distracted limbs.
Their shame is ours. We, too, are haunted by their fate.

In the shock of flame, their tears brand our flesh,
We twist in their furnace, and our scorching throats
Parch for the waters where the cool dead float.
We press our lips upon the river where they drink, and drown.

Their voices call to us, in pain and indignation:
'This is what you have done to us!'
—Their accusation is our final hope. Be comforted.
Yes, we have heard you, ghosts of our indifference,

We hear your cry, we understand your warnings.
We, too, shall refuse to accept our fate!
Haunt us with the truth of our betrayal
Until the earth's united voices shout refusal, sing your peace!

Forgive us, that we had to see your passion to remember
What we must never again deny: *Love one another.*

NO MORE HIROSHIMAS

At the station exit, my bundle in hand,
Early the winter afternoon's wet snow
Falls thinly round me, out of a crudded sun.
I had forgotten to remember where I was.
Looking about, I see it might be anywhere—
A station, a town like any other in Japan,
Ramshackle, muddy, noisy, drab; a cheerfully
Shallow permanence: peeling concrete, litter, 'Atomic
Lotion, for hair fall-out,' a flimsy department-store;
Racks and towers of neon, flashy over tiled and tilted waves
Of little roofs, shacks cascading lemons and persimmons,
Oranges and dark-red apples, shanties awash with rainbows
Of squid and octopus, shellfish, slabs of tuna, oysters, ice,
Ablaze with fans of soiled nude-picture books
Thumbed abstractedly by schoolboys, with second-hand looks.

The river remains unchanged, sad, refusing rehabilitation.
In this long, wide, empty official boulevard
The new trees are still small, the office blocks
Basely functional, the bridge a slick abstraction.
But the river remains unchanged, sad, refusing rehabilitation.

In the city centre, far from the station's lively squalor,
A kind of life goes on, in cinemas and hi-fi coffee bars,
In the shuffling racket of pin-table palaces and parlours,
The souvenir-shops piled with junk, kimonoed kewpie-dolls,
Models of the bombed Industry Promotion Hall, memorial ruin
Tricked out with glitter-frost and artificial pearls.

Set in an awful emptiness, the modern tourist hotel is trimmed
With jaded Christmas frippery, flatulent balloons; in the hall,
A giant dingy iced cake in the shape of a Cinderella coach.
The contemporary stairs are treacherous, the corridors
Deserted, my room an overheated morgue, the bar in darkness.
Punctually, the electric chimes ring out across the tidy waste
Their doleful public hymn—the tune unrecognisable, evangelist.

Here atomic peace is geared to meet the tourist trade.
Let it remain like this, for all the world to see,
Without nobility or loveliness, and dogged with shame
That is beyond all hope of indignation. Anger, too, is dead.
And why should memorials of what was far
From pleasant have the grace that helps us to forget?

In the dying afternoon, I wander dying round the Park of
    Peace.
It is right, this squat, dead place, with its left-over air
Of an abandoned International Trade and Tourist Fair.
The stunted trees are wrapped in straw against the cold.
The gardeners are old, old women in blue bloomers, white
    aprons,
Survivors weeding the dead brown lawns around the Children's
    Monument.

A hideous pile, the Atomic Bomb Explosion Centre, freezing
    cold,
'Includes the Peace Tower, a museum containing
Atomic-melted slates and bricks, photos showing
What the Atomic Desert looked like, and other
Relics of the catastrophe.'

The other relics:
The ones that made me weep;
The bits of burnt clothing,
The stopped watches, the torn shirts.
The twisted buttons,
The stained and tattered vests and drawers,
The ripped kimonos and charred boots,
The white blouse polka-dotted with atomic rain, indelible,
The cotton summer pants the blasted boys crawled home in,
    to bleed
And slowly die.

Remember only these.
They are the memorials we need.

EARTHQUAKE

An old man's flamingo-coloured kite
Twitches higher over tiled roofs.
Idly gazing through the metal gauze
That nets the winter sun beyond my sliding windows,
I notice that all the telegraph-poles along the lane
Are waggling convulsively, and the wires
Bounce like skipping-ropes round flustered birds.
The earth creeps under the floor. A cherry tree
Agitates itself outside, but it is no wind
That makes the long bamboo palisade
Begin to undulate down all its length.

The clock stammers and stops. There is a queer racket,
Like someone rapping on the wooden walls,
Then through the ceiling's falling flakes I see
The brass handles on a high chest of drawers
Dithering and dancing in a brisk distraction.
The lamp swings like a headache, and the whole house
Rotates slightly on grinding rollers.
Smoothly, like a spoilt child putting out a tongue,
A drawer shoots half-out, and quietly glides back again,
Closed with a snap of teeth, a sharper click
Than such a casual grimace prepared me for.

The stove-pipe's awkward elbow
Twangles its three supporting wires. Doors
Slam, fly open: my quiet maid erupts from
Nowhere, blushing furiously, yet smiling wildly
As if to explain, excuse, console and warn.
Together, like lost children in a fairy-tale
Who escape from an enchanter's evil cottage,
We rush out into the slightly unbalanced garden. A pole
Vibrates still like a plucked bass string,
But the ground no longer squirms beneath our feet,
And the trees are composing themselves, have birds again.

In the spooky quiet, a 'plane drones
Like a metal top, and though the sound
Gives a sense of disaster averted,
And is even oddly re-assuring, as
The pulse of confident engines,
Throbbing high above an electric storm, can comfort,
We feel that somewhere out of sight
Something has done its worst. Meanwhile,
The house tries to look as if nothing had happened,
And over the roof's subtle curves
Lets the flamingo-coloured kite fly undisturbed.

THE SUBMERGED VILLAGE

Calm, the surrounding mountains look upon
the steeple's golden cross, that still
emerges from the centre of the rising lake.
Like a sinking raft's bare mast and spar,
anchored to earth by chains of stone and the unbreaking
ropes of death, it stands alone, becalmed.

No other evidences now remain
of what was once a village in the plain.

A fitful bell bangs in the belfry's suffocating tank.
In the churchyard, vaults and tombs burst open with dead
gusts of air, and coffins, single-manned, are launched
like death-ships over the yews now green for ever.
The wave-packed windows darken, leak and spring apart.
Dead as the drowning wind, the centuries of prayer
sink with the stifling sands, that drift through doors
and wave-picked locks like fine draughts over heaving floors.

What were the feelings of the wild springs, the sweet
wells that without warning began to feel themselves
rising, filled with an overwhelming dread?
The kitchen sinks flowed over to the ceiling, as if some
careless hand had turned on all the taps, and left them running;
and startled, homely ponds felt all their fences falling
and their natures changing as their growing shores contained
more mysteries than their simplicity could comprehend.

Among those stilled streets, those scentless lanes
whose summer blossoming is melted like their snow, whose spring
leaves are blasted in a forest of profounder green;
and on the bridle-paths that led the trustful fields
from gate to gate, and down the leisurely, confiding hedge;
where gates swing now at the current's arm, and hedges blow
in a strange season's gales and breezes, what inhabitants
are left to guard and memorise their native haunts?

Only those who can inhale like mountain air
the breathless waters of another land, another time,
live there. With dumb yawns the gloomy fishes glide, and flash
like flocks of silent starlings through the trees too full
of tears for weeping: they never knew so dense a rain, and drop
soundlessly their autumn's long, uncounted leaves
upon the mossy roads no sun will ever dry,
for fate's heavy cloud upon them is their only sky.

And even ghostlier than these, the ghosts themselves
return, and are so troubled by the single change
they feel more ghostly even than they are,
poor ghosts of what was once a life, a house, a bed
breathing and warm with sleep, alight with love;
poor ghosts, lost in the presence of a fatal memory,

remembering a room, a table, a window and a stream
as if they were eternity, and not this unremembered dream!

Now, phantoms too, and brief observers following the new
mountain road that like a vivid scar cuts the contained
fury of those dark and gleaming heights,
it is we, and not the birds alone, those sure, far climbers,
who stand with fall-dreaming pride, look down upon
that sign of mercy once looked up to from our knees below.
Travelling with cloud-shadows down the unnatural pass,
we see its last reflection, inverted in the faithless glass.

THE BOWL OF GOLDFISH: A FABLE

To make the best of Fate's inordinate demands
Should be our hope, for Fate's the final master;
But to ignore his ineluctable commands
Precipitates, as we shall see, a self-induced disaster.

Good Noah left behind him, when he launched the Ark,
A bowl of goldfish, three that had long deplored
The limitations of a life so circumspect.
'We're *buried* in this dull provincial watering-place,'
They all would groan. And, though their water frequently was
      changed,
They said it was stagnation, with the same old faces all the time.
'We're always bumping into one another,' they would moan.
'We'd rather tarnish in some quaint cathedral town;
For there, at least, one has the salt of scandal: one can escape,
      what's more,
To the comparative metropolis of a department-store.
But here, we've found, all is not gold that glitters, when there's
      iron in the soul:
Two's company, perhaps, but three's a *shoal!*'

Wise Noah then assured them, when the Deluge came,
They would at least be in their element again.
'*Après toi, le Déluge,*' they mournfully predicted,
And hid their glee. Then to the household cats they waved a fond
Adieu, flicking their fins in sunny lamentations,
And warmed their glassy confines with golden speculations.

The Deluge came. And, as they had foreseen,
That El Dorado, an eternal, rounded rim,

93

From an air-sealed entrance to a wave-sprung exit changed.
Amid the mounting flood, their gold-rimmed eyes looked out
Upon the rising waters from the porthole of a globe
That caged their lesser sea, a home from home, no doubt,
All windows, too—but it had cabined them too long.
Alas! they stared dumbfounded, when other fishes, monsters,
Merest dross, swam sullenly, with vulgar curiosity, around
The smooth correctness of their snug conservatory,
As if they themselves, not those of baser metal,
Were queer fish in some subaqueous observatory!

Now fish in glass houses must not throw stones;
Still, a privacy had been invaded, they felt it in their bones!
So, like a famous actor resting, each put on his private face,
And delicately drew down weeds, as a marine velarium
Against the importunity of gazes public as the sun, the deep
        disgrace
Of being taken for a commonplace aquarium.

In vain! For when the outrageous waters reached
That prison-portal circumscribed by nothing like an O,
Each linking ocean, turning in the other like a key,
By interlocking loosed their wards; and golden prisoners
That long had chafed against a wall they could not see
Unwillingly escaped, were elevated from their proper station
And immediately floated in the same sad element.
But sadder, wilder, rougher, more immense
This terrifying, finite informality than was
Their former comfortably infinite and formal O!
Lost, lost in the shapeless oceans of their foolish wish
Like sparks of fire they flashed, and were extinguished, fish
        by fish!

One in the gloomy cemeteries of a cold and salty deep,
One into a shark's vast maw departed, both
Like gilded butterflies distracted in a cave of endless dark.
An enormous catfish, out of nowhere sprung,
Swallowed the third (*aurum potabile*), with no apparent relish.
Those teeth! Those blazing eyes! Alas, poor fish! poor fish!
        poor fish!

To make the best of Fate's inordinate demands
Should be our hope, for Fate's the final master;
But to ignore his ineluctable commands
Precipitates, as we have seen, a self-induced disaster.

A CITY OF THE NORTH

Out of green andy ston dales, where, like enormous dice,
The grey, black-windowed mills are cast, in time's
Improbable design, across the grassy tables of a game
That once was innocent; out of the heavy air, the slow
And slower darknesses of the corrupted river

That was once a stream, pure as the sky it leapt from,
But that now sinks through the city to the manufactories
Of earth, and the continual transformations of the sea:
Out of bare rock and hard land, out of the wildness
Of the crude and solitary fell, the cultivated city rose.

A rare sun comments on the most important buildings
With a frankness that does not dismay
Their self-approval, based upon a proper consciousness
Of solid worth, and industry rewarded, as it can be,
With what it often least deserves, a kind of dignity.

An imposing front is what successful business needs.
And so the architecture of a lesser age, Grand
Concourse (L.M.S.) and Civic Hall and University and smart
       hotel,
Sepulchres all, all whited more or less, display their bland
Exteriors, sleek stone façades betraying honest brick behind.

Rhetorical, the *haute école* performers on their public plinth
Make a convenience of the city square, and architectural profusion
Where Pugin's little church, all crocketed and cramped,
Unwillingly presides, with patience in a grassy garden waits,
While green 'buses lean outside, and linger proudly on their
       screaming brakes.

In summer limned by doves, in winter by the charming snow,
The Town Hall's noble blacknesses appal, a great
Berg of pillared stone and plunging steps, where four
Grey lions with rain-eroded flanks bare toothless jaws,
Glare out of soot-stained masks over their blunted paws.

A hard rain stubbles the rooftops and the streets,
But still the patient queues are standing
Outside the cinemas, those other, darker mills,
Where other shadows work, and love, and violently die.
Acid neon bites and burns, a universal branding.

Let us all ride a capering tram to Temple Newsam,
To where we can smell the quiet dales again, and see
The total heaven of a clearer sky, a larger day!
Where the truly permanent invades a temporary way,
And steel rails in the trampled grass

Rise, shining like a stream,
Out of the terminus beneath intransitory trees.

A VISIT TO BRONTËLAND

The road climbs from the valley past the public
Park and turns, at the Haworth Co-operative Stores,
Into the grey stone village, and the steep
Street leading to the Parsonage, the Inn, the W.C.s;
To the Church of St. Michael and All Angels, high in trees.

The West Lane Baptists are putting on
Patience, the playbills say. The Heathcliffe Tearooms are aglow
With English teachers in sensible tweeds. Bearded cyclists
Lean on their pedals, and their saddles shine and sway
Up the hill to the Y.H.A.

Across the valley thick with mills
The fellside rises like an aerial map
Of fields and drystone walls and farms.
Pylons saunter over with a minimum of fuss,
And round the bend from Keighley comes the Brontë 'bus.

An arty signboard poses Charlotte in a crinoline
And ringlets, penning *Jane Eyre*, at a table, with a quill.
'This must be *it*'.—The wondering Americans, like Technicolor
    ads.,
Have reverence plainly written on their open faces.
They know just how one should behave in hallowed places.

A sea of scriptured slabs
Shines in the graveyard under the twilight rain.
The cold winds are crying in the trees.
New heights above the pines
Are wuthered by tractors of open-cast mines.

The church where the Brontës worshipped
Is long demolished. Only a brass plate

Marks where their bones are buried. Smothered
In Parks Committee geraniums, Anne lies alone
In Scarborough Old Churchyard, under a dolled-up stone.

Now, in the village roofs, the television aerial aspires.
No idle toy would have tempted Branwell
From the 'Bull', and brandy; or kept that sister
From her tragic poems. They knew they had nothing but the
    moor
And themselves. It is we, who want all, who are poor.

TO THE ANCESTRAL NORTH

I

From that elemental land
Of iron whitenesses and long auroras
My Viking fathers sprang
In armoured nakedness.
The rock rang, and cold fire
Sparked at their striding heels.
Their prows plundered and struck the up-
Ending northern oceans with the smash
Of sword on stone, axe
Biting the pale flesh of the dark pines.
The wintered masts were holy,
Bore flame and fire from the gods,
And all Valhalla thundered in the mystic storm.

II

I love the archaic North,
The gothic loneliness,
The bare cathedral of the cold
Where, in the stunned ice,
The winter woods display
A stripped elegance, and frame the rare
Rose-window of the midnight sun.

III

There, in the blank fastnesses
Of frozen bays, on sands
Sheeted with stony ice,
By the frost-pleated firth, the glassy

Fjord scattered with ashes of snows;
Under the sea-mountain
In the wild moraine of stars
That haul the glazed oceans into heaps
Of shaggy ice, the ancestral ghosts
Of gods and heroes wander,
Melancholy, silent, and remote.

IV

O in the cold and grave and Carolingian forest,
In epic stillness, let me worship in their memory
The falling flake, the long
Larch grove, the lime-white lake
That burns in the trees' black lancets!

The twilight pauses like a stag at bay.
I hear a lost huntsman calling for a hidden castle.
And in the deserted valley
A sad horn echoes in a last, lingering *hallali*.

FOR THE 90TH BIRTHDAY OF SIBELIUS

8th December, 1955

You are the old, the violent and melancholy master of that final
        land,
Where, down the sky's large whitenesses, the archipelagoes of day
Gradually move, on forests light with birch and black with larch,
In grave progressions, all the silent masses of the hanging snows.

There the ancestral stillness pulses with the beat of high
Oceans hammering unalterable shores, and shivers with leagues
Of light-sheeted lakes baring their wide reflections to a wind
That greys their elemental pallor with the dark of stone.

A land of quiet marches, where the estuaries of the constant day
Spread vast, ethereal and cold in the remoteness of the sun,
And air teems with the waterfalling shade of clouds and wings;
A land of mysterious natural sounds and thunderous pauses.

Here muted horns blow sharp and small as human cries
Over the ground of ocean, over the groined land brooding in male
Slumber. Under the generating spells of ice and sand
Firm winter holds in moody restlessness the seed

Of rock and iron, the fertile germ of energy, abundant, wild.
All quivers in the drum-deep thrall, the whispering suspension
Of supernatural breath: a poised avalanche trembles on a thrusting
    root
That groans and rustles in the dark, whose trumpet splits the
    cataracts of sleep.

Now a distant horse and rider flicker through the running trees;
A hero stirs, and tramples the ice along the river's edge. In mid
Night, men and horses lean to the festive ploughs;
Black boughs dance with birds, and the birds are leaves.

—May you, too, austere and stern and legendary master,
Feel always in the age of earth the gathering Spring,
And see the new leaves lifted on a flight of swans,
And hear again the music of the air, the ocean and the earth

Release their gay eternities from grief and wrong—
And let the Winter move you always with its hidden song.

RUGBY LEAGUE GAME

Sport is absurd, and sad.
Those grown men, just look,
In those dreary long blue shorts,
Those ringed stockings, Edwardian,
Balding pates, and huge
Fat knees that ought to be heroes'.

Grappling, hooking, gallantly tackling—
Is all this courage really necessary?—
Taking their good clean fun
So solemnly, they run each other down
With earnest keenness, for the honour of
Virility, the cap, the county side.

Like great boys they roll each other
In the mud of public Saturdays,
Groping their blind way back
To noble youth, away from the bank,
The wife, the pram, the spin drier,
Back to the Spartan freedom of the field.

Back, back to the days when boys
Were men, still hopeful, and untamed.
That was then: a gay
And golden age ago.
Now, in vain, domesticated,
Men try to be boys again.

TO AN OLD LADY ASLEEP AT A POETRY
READING

Snore on in your front-row chair! Let not my voice
Disturb the wordless heaven that your eyes have found!
I, too, would welcome that release,
Here in this hard hall with the naked lights
In which my spirit and my words are bound,
The nightmare setting of all sleepless nights.

Why do the others, too, not briefly doze?
My voice has laid a healthy spell
Upon your gentle fret, and on a mind that glows
Still with a small but vivid fire.
They surely felt the moderate enchantment just as well?
Why do we all not sleep, abandoning these platforms that do
        more than tire?

Dear lady, do not let that wakeful vulture,
Your tiresome neighbour, provoke you with her nudging gloom.
She is one of those restless seekers after culture,
Guardians of Beauty who at Question-time will always shout
        for it,
While I desire only the chilly sanctuary of the chairman's
        guestroom.
Let her be in on everything: you're better out of it!

Poor dear, she's wakened you. The sweet sleep sours.
Snug in your old fur-coat, you stare
Perplexed a moment, from under your hat's provincial flowers.
—You must not mind, old girl, as shame comes hunting you:
Try to preserve, as I do, this unruffled air . . .
Yes, dear, this is hell, and this is me confronting you.

TEA IN A SPACE-SHIP

In this world a tablecloth need not be laid
On any table, but is spread out anywhere
Upon the always equidistant and
Invisible legs of gravity's wild air.

The tea, which never would grow cold,
Gathers itself into a wet and steaming ball,
And hurls its liquid molecules at anybody's head,
Or dances, eternal bilboquet,
In and out of the suspended cups up-
Ended in the weightless hands
Of chronically nervous jerks
Who yet would never spill a drop,
Their mouths agape for passing cakes.

Lumps of sparkling sugar
Sling themselves out of their crystal bowl
With a disordered fountain's
Ornamental stops and starts.
The milk describes a permanent parabola
Girdled with satellites of spinning tarts.

The future lives with graciousness.
The hostess finds her problems eased,
For there is honey still for tea
And butter keeps the ceiling greased.

She will provide, of course,
No cake-forks, spoons or knives.
They are so sharp, so dangerously gadabout,
It is regarded as a social misdemeanour
To put them out.

THE SHEPHERD'S TALE

From the French of Raoul Ponchon

Woman, you'll never credit what
    My two eyes saw this night . . .
But first of all we'll have a drop,
    It's freezing now, all right.

It was the queerest going-on
    That I did e'er behold:
A holy child out in the barn,
    A baby all in gold.

Now let's get started on the soup,
    And let me tell it you,
For though there's not a thing made up,
    It still seems hardly true.

There he was laid upon the straw,
    Will you dish up the stew?
The ass did bray, the hens did craw,
    I'll have some cabbage too.

First there was a king from Prussia,
    At least that's how he looked,
Then there was the king of Russia.
    This stew's been overcooked.

There they were kneeling on the ground.
    Come, have a bite to eat.
First I just stared and stood around.
    Have just a taste of meat!

Well, one of them he ups and says
    A long speech—kind of funny.
Here, what about that last new cheese,
    Is it still runny?

The little 'un, wise as wise could be,
    Just didn't care for that.
But he was pleased as punch with me
    When I took off me hat.

I took his little fists in mine,
    In front of all those nobs.
Fetch us a jug of our best wine
    My dear, we'll wet our gobs.

That very instant, as if I'd
    Had a good swig of drink,
I felt a great warm joy inside,
    But why, I cannot think.

Ah, this wine's the stuff, by Mary!
  When he's grown up a bit,
That little fellow, just you see,
  He shall have some of it!

We might have all been knelt there yet,
  Put a Yule log on the fire,
But suddenly he starts to fret—
  He'd begun to tire.

Then 'Sirs', his mother she did say,
  'It grieves me to remind
You that it's time to go away
  When you have been so kind.

'But see, how sleepy he's become,
  He's crying, let him rest.
You all know how to find our home
  Each one's a welcome guest.'

And so in silence we went out,
  But the funniest thing—
Those three fine kings, so rich and stout,
  Did wish me good-morning!

You see, love, that's how it began.
  The God born on the earth
This night's no ordinary one.
  Let's celebrate his birth!

A CHARM FOR THE EAR-ACHE

Now let music, light as an enchanter's hands,
And warm and fragrant as a summer's air
Be gently breathed into this anxious ear.
Then, like a magic ointment, or fine sands
Of coral drowsed by an ocean's golden suns,
Let all wild sounds in quiet poems come
To charm the angry drum with murmured monotones.
Now let the face of love lift from a dream
His gravely smiling lips, and silent lay
Their honeyed wisdom here! O, let the tongue
With healing science harmonise my long
Discordances, and kiss all wakefulness at last away!

Laurie Lee

Introduction

Laurie Lee was born in Stroud, Gloucestershire, and lived for the first twenty years of his life in the nearby village of Slad. He was the youngest but one of a family of eight, and was educated at the local village school and at Stroud Central School, which he left at the age of fifteen.

During his teens he ran the local dance band before leaving home to seek his fortune, walking to London—a journey which took him a month—where he got a job as a builder's labourer. He was in Spain when the Civil War broke out, and returned there a year later by walking across the Pyrenees. In 1938–9 he also visited the eastern Mediterranean, spending some time in Greece and Cyprus.

During the Second World War he made documentary films for the G.P.O. Film Unit and others, travelling as a scriptwriter to Cyprus, India and Assam. In 1951 he was awarded the M.B.E. for his work as Curator of Eccentricities at the Festival of Britain Exhibition in London.

This selection includes poems from all three of Laurie Lee's collections of verse. His first book, published in 1944, naturally contains many poems arising from his war experiences: 'Seafront' is inspired by the barbed wire entanglements erected along our coasts and tells of mankind watching

> through the black sights of a gun
> the winging flocks of migratory birds
> who cannot speak of freedom, yet are free.

'The Long War' ends ironically:

> But as our twisted arms embrace
> the desert where our cities stood,
> death's family likeness in each face
> must show, at last, our brotherhood.

But Mr Lee's 'war' poems are but a small part of his verse. He gives us pictures of places he has visited in such poems as 'Bombay

Arrival' and 'Stork in Jerez', pictures made vivid by his use of imagery which is reminiscent of the Metaphysical poets:

> Slow-hooved across the carrion sea,
> Smeared by the betel-spitting sun,
> Like cows the Bombay islands come
> Dragging the mainland into view.

and

> The dhow upon its shadow clings—
> A dark moth pinioned to the day.

C. V. Wedgwood has said: 'There is nothing slack or vague in his poetry; the more startling or fanciful the vision, the more firm and exact the words in which it is expressed. At his best he involves the reader with him completely in the intensity of the captured moment.' In 'Home from Abroad' his language is particularly well chosen: he returns from abroad, his skin 'well-oiled with wines of the Levant . . . to greet the pale, domestic kiss of Kent'. But 'that gawky girl, recalled so primly' while he was overseas, surprises him with her gifts—'her rolling tidal landscape, . . . simple horses, . . . roses fat as cream'.

Included in this selection are many of Laurie Lee's 'nature' poems; they range widely in subject matter and feeling, from 'April Rise' with its 'blessing in the air' to 'Field of Autumn'—

> Slow moves the hour that sucks our life,
> slow drops the late wasp from the flower,
> the rose tree's thread of scent draws thin—
> and snaps upon the air.

Apart from his books of verse, Mr Lee has written a radio play, *The Voyage of Magellan*, a travel book on Spain, and his auto-biography, *Cider with Rosie*.

MY MANY-COATED MAN

Under the scarlet-licking leaves,
through bloody thought and bubbly shade,
the padded, spicy tiger moves—
a sheath of swords, a hooded blade.

The turtle on the naked sand
peels to the air his pewter snout
and rubs the sky with slotted shell—
the heart's dismay turned inside out.

The rank red fox goes forth at night
to bite the gosling's downy throat,
then digs his grave with panic claws
to share oblivion with the stoat.

The mottled moth, pinned to a tree,
woos with his wings the bark's disease
and strikes a fungoid, fevered pose
to live forgotten and at ease.

Like these, my many-coated man
shields his hot hunger from the wind,
and, hooded by a smile, commits
his private murder in the mind.

SUNKEN EVENING

The green light floods the city square—
    A sea of fowl and feathered fish,
    Where squalls of rainbirds dive and splash
And gusty sparrows chop the air.

Submerged, the prawn-blue pigeons feed
    In sandy grottoes round the Mall,
    And crusted lobster-buses crawl
Among the fountains' silver weed.

There, like a wreck, with mast and bell,
    The torn church settles by the bow,
    While phosphorescent starlings stow
'Their mussel shells along the hull.

The oyster-poet, drowned but dry,
    Rolls a black pearl between his bones;
    The typist, trapped by telephones,
Gazes in bubbles at the sky.

Till, with the dark, the shallows run,
    And homeward surges tide and fret—
    The slow night trawls its heavy net
And hauls the clerk to Surbiton.

BOMBAY ARRIVAL

Slow-hooved across the carrion sea,
Smeared by the betel-spitting sun,
Like cows the Bombay islands come
Dragging the mainland into view.

The loose flank loops the rocky bone,
The light beats thin on horn and hill;
Still breeds the flesh for hawks, and still
The Hindu heart drips on a stone.

Around the wide dawn-ridden bay
The waters move their daggered wings;
The dhow upon its shadow clings—
A dark moth pinioned to the day.

False in the morning, screened with silk,
Neat as an egg the Town draws near,
False as a map her streets appear
Ambling, and odourless as milk.

Until she holds us face to face—
A crumbling mask with bullet pores,
A nakedness of jewels and sores
Clutched with our guilt in her embrace.

SCOT IN THE DESERT

All day the sand, like golden chains,
The desert distance binds;
All day the crouching camels groan,
Whipped by the gritty winds.

The mountain, flayed by sun, reveals
Red muscles, wounds of stone,
While on its face the black goats swarm
And bite it to the bone.

Here light is death; on every rock
It stretches like a cry,
Its fever burns up every bush,
It drinks each river dry.

It cracks with thirst the creviced lip,
It fattens black the tongue,
It turns the storm cloud into dust,
The morning dew to dung.

Men were not made to flourish here,
They shroud their heads and fly—
Save one, who stares into the sun
With sky-blue British eye.

Who stares into the zenith sun
And smiles and feels no pain,
Blood-cooled by Calvin, mist and bog,
And summers in the rain.

HOME FROM ABROAD

Far-fetched with tales of other worlds and ways,
My skin well-oiled with wines of the Levant,
I set my face into a filial smile
To greet the pale, domestic kiss of Kent.

But shall I never learn? That gawky girl,
Recalled so primly in my foreign thoughts,
Becomes again the green-haired queen of love
Whose wanton form dilates as it delights.

Her rolling tidal landscape floods the eye
And drowns Chianti in a dusky stream;
The flower-flecked grasses swim with simple horses,
The hedges choke with roses fat as cream.

So do I breathe the hayblown airs of home,
And watch the sea-green elms drip birds and shadows,
And as the twilight nets the plunging sun
My heart's keel slides to rest among the meadows.

SEAFRONT

Here like the maze of our bewilderment
the thorn-crowned wire spreads high along the shore,
and flowers with rust, and tears our common sun;
and where no paths of love may reach the sea
the shut sands wait deserted for the drowned.

On other islands similarly barbed
mankind lies self-imprisoned in his fear,
and watches through the black sights of a gun
the winging flocks of migratory birds
who cannot speak of freedom, yet are free.

THE LONG WAR

Less passionate the long war throws
its burning thorn about all men,
caught in one grief, we share one wound,
and cry one dialect of pain.

We have forgot who fired the house,
whose easy mischief spilt first blood,
under one raging roof we lie
the fault no longer understood.

But as our twisted arms embrace
the desert where our cities stood,
death's family likeness in each face
must show, at last, our brotherhood.

APRIL RISE

If ever I saw blessing in the air
  I see it now in this still early day
Where lemon-green the vaporous morning drips
  Wet sunlight on the powder of my eye.

Blown bubble-film of blue, the sky wraps round
  Weeds of warm light whose every root and rod
Splutters with soapy green, and all the world
  Sweats with the bead of summer in its bud.

If ever I heard blessing it is there
  Where birds in trees that shoals and shadows are
Splash with their hidden wings and drops of sound
  Break on my ears their crests of throbbing air.

Pure in the haze the emerald sun dilates,
  The lips of sparrows milk the mossy stones,
While white as water by the lake a girl
  Swims her green hand among the gathered swans.

Now, as the almond burns its smoking wick,
  Dropping small flames to light the candled grass;
Now, as my low blood scales its second chance,
  If ever world were blessed, now it is.

THE THREE WINDS

The hard blue winds of March
shake the young sheep
and flake the long stone walls;
now from the gusty grass
comes the horned music of rams,
and plovers fall out of the sky
filling their wings with snow.

Tired of this northern tune
the winds turn soft
blowing white butterflies
out of the dog-rose hedges,
and schoolroom songs are full
of boy's green cuckoos
piping the summer round

Till August sends at last
its brick-red breath
over the baking wheat and blistered poppy,
brushing with feathered hands
the skies of brass,
with dreams of river moss
my thirst's delirium.

FIELD OF AUTUMN

Slow moves the acid breath of noon
over the copper-coated hill,
slow from the wild crab's bearded breast
the palsied apples fall.

Like coloured smoke the day hangs fire,
taking the village without sound;
the vulture-headed sun lies low
chained to the violet ground.

The horse upon the rocky height
rolls all the valley in his eye,
but dares not raise his foot or move
his shoulders from the fly.

The sheep, snail-backed against the wall,
lifts her blind face but does not know
the cry her blackened tongue gives forth
is the first bleat of snow.

Each bird and stone, each roof and well,
feels the gold foot of autumn pass;
each spider binds with glittering snare
the splintered bones of grass.

Slow moves the hour that sucks our life,
slow drops the late wasp from the flower,
the rose tree's thread of scent draws thin——
and snaps upon the air.

APPLES

Behold the apples' rounded worlds:
juice-green of July rain,
the black polestar of flowers, the rind
mapped with its crimson stain.

The russet, crab and cottage red
burn to the sun's hot brass,
then drop like sweat from every branch
and bubble in the grass.

They lie as wanton as they fall,
and where they fall and break,
the stallion clamps his crunching jaws,
the starling stabs his beak.

In each plump gourd the cidery bite
of boys' teeth tears the skin;
the waltzing wasp consumes his share,
the bent worm enters in.

I, with as easy hunger, take
entire my season's dole;
welcome the ripe, the sweet, the sour,
the hollow and the whole.

STORK IN JEREZ

White-arched in loops of silence, the bodega
Lies drowsed in spices, where the antique woods
Piled in solera, dripping years of flavour,
Distil their golden fumes among the shades.

In from the yard—where barrels under fig-trees
Split staves of sunlight from the noon's hot glare—
The tall stork comes; black-stilted, sagely witted,
Wiping his careful beak upon the air.

He is a priest-like presence, he inscribes
Sharp as a pen his staid and written dance,
Skating the floor with stiffened plumes behind him,
Gravely off-balance, solemn in his trance.

Drunk on these sherry vapours, eyes akimbo,
He treads among the casks, makes a small leap,
Flaps wildly, fails to fly—until at last,
Folded umbrella-wise, he falls asleep.

So bird and bard exchange their spheres of pleasure:
He, from his high-roofed nest now levelled lies;
Whilst I, earth-tied, breathing these wines take wing
And float amazed across his feathered skies.

TOWN OWL

On eves of cold, when slow coal fires,
rooted in basements, burn and branch,
brushing with smoke the city air;

When quartered moons pale in the sky,
and neons glow along the dark
like deadly nightshade on a briar;

Above the muffled traffic then
I hear the owl, and at his note
I shudder in my private chair.

For like an augur he has come
to roost among our crumbling walls,
his blooded talons sheathed in fur.

Some secret lure of time it seems
has called him from his country wastes
to hunt a newer wasteland here.

And where the candelabra swung
bright with the dancers' thousand eyes,
now his black, hooded pupils stare,

And where the silk-shoed lovers ran
with dust of diamonds in their hair,
he opens now his silent wing,

And, like a stroke of doom, drops down,
and swoops across the empty hall,
and plucks a quick mouse off the stair . . .

COCK-PHEASANT

Gilded with leaf-thick paint; a steady
Eye fixed like a ruby rock;
Across the cidrous banks of autumn
Swaggers the stamping pheasant-cock.

The thrusting nut and bursting apple
Accompany his jointed walk,
The creviced pumpkin and the marrow
Bend to his path on melting stalk.

Sure as an Inca priest or devil,
Feathers stroking down the corn,
He blinks the lively dust of daylight,
Blind to the hunter's powder-horn.

For me, alike, this flushed October—
Ripe, and round-fleshed, and bellyful—
Fevers me fast but cannot fright, though
Each dropped leaf shows the winter's skull.

CHRISTMAS LANDSCAPE

Tonight the wind gnaws
with teeth of glass,
the jackdaw shivers
in caged branches of iron,
the stars have talons.

There is hunger in the mouth
of vole and badger,
silver agonies of breath
in the nostril of the fox,
ice on the rabbit's paw.

Tonight has no moon,
no food for the pilgrim;
the fruit tree is bare,
the rose bush a thorn
and the ground bitter with stones.

But the mole sleeps, and the hedghog
lies curled in a womb of leaves,
the bean and the wheat-seed
hug their germs in the earth
and the stream moves under the ice.

Tonight there is no moon,
but a new star opens
like a silver trumpet over the dead.
Tonight in a nest of ruins
the blessed babe is laid.

And the fir tree warms to a bloom of candles,
the child lights his lantern,
stares at his tinselled toy;
our hearts and hearths
smoulder with live ashes.

In the blood of our grief
the cold earth is suckled,
in our agony the womb
convulses its seed,
in the cry of anguish
the child's first breath is born.

Norman Nicholson

The only biographical information which is of any real use to readers of my poetry is the fact that I was born in 1914 at Millom in Cumberland. Both my parents belonged there before me, and I have lived ever since in the house where I was born. Such a stick-in-the-mud life is unusual in present-day England, at least among the kind of people who become poets. Had all been well, in fact, I would have trained for a profession and would probably have spent my life moving from post to post and town to town throughout the north of England. But all was not well, and at the age of sixteen I was taken seriously ill and spent nearly two years in bed—this is the period referred to in the poem called 'The Pot Geranium'. When I came home I was forced, for a long while, to put aside all thoughts of leaving Millom, and to settle down to a quiet, restricted and, it would seem, extremely hum-drum existence.

Yet it was precisely this which turned me into a poet. At first I resented it. I hated the drab little industrial town in which I was living. I tried to escape, whenever I could, into the hills of the Lake District, or into the countryside of fields, woods, heath, the marshes of the Duddon Estuary and the sands of the Cumberland coast which lay close at hand. Gradually I came to realise that my real roots were even closer—in the very town I had been pretending to despise. I saw the iron ore mines and the blast furnaces and realised that the life and livelihood of the people depended on the rock every bit as much as the livelihood of a farmer depends on the soil. For though Millom is an industrial town, we who live in it are really living on the land. In fact, that is true of everybody alive on earth, whether they belong to a city of eight million inhabitants or whether they are alone on a desert island. Only if you do live in a city it is hard to remember this—hard to remember that the food out of tins and the milk out of bottles and all the steel, glass and concrete of the skyscrapers come out of the soil and the rock to begin with. In Millom you just can't forget, for you see the whole process laid out in front of you. You see the ore come out of the mines; you see it carried across to the blast furnaces. And you see it come out of the furnaces, not just as pig iron, to go to the making of steel, but as money, to go to the making of homes and the shaping of human lives.

It is perhaps this human dimension that matters most to me. In the great cities people cease to belong to a recognizable community, and the poet or the artist becomes a man set apart from other men. But if I tried to pretend that I was a man set apart I would soon be put in my place. I can scarcely walk down a single street of Millom without meeting someone to whom I'm related—my father had thirteen brothers, so that, as a boy, I had no lack of uncles. When there is a strike or a stoppage at the mines or the furnaces, what worries me is not that the unemployment figures go up, but that men I have known all my life, men I went to school with, are now out of work. Human society, to me, is not a matter of politics or social movements, but a matter of people, and of people I know. That is why, though I may seem to be writing about an out-of-date town and an old-fashioned community, I am really writing about the essentials of human life as it is lived everywhere.

Of course, much of the time I write about just what happens to catch my fancy: rivers, lakes, quarries, weeds, back-streets, chapels, cricket matches. Sometimes I get well away from Millom. 'Windscale' tells of the occasion when there was a radioactive leak at the atomic power station of Calder Hall, twenty miles up the Cumberland coast. 'Gathering Sticks on Sunday' is about the Man in the Moon, who, according to my grandmother, was sent there for breaking the laws of the Sabbath. (He is also the man condemned to death by Moses in *Numbers*, xv, 32–36.)

THE UNDISCOVERED PLANET

Out on the furthest tether let it run
Its hundred-year-long orbit, cold
As solid mercury, old and dead
Before this world's fermenting bread
Had got a crust to cover it; landscape of lead
Whose purple voes and valleys are
Lit faintly by a sun
No nearer than a measurable star.

No man has seen it; the lensed eye
That pin-points week by week the same patch of sky
Records not even a blur across its pupil; only
The errantry of Saturn, the wry
Retarding of Uranus, speak
Of the pull beyond the pattern:
The unknown is shown
Only by a bend in the known.

THE EXPANDING UNIVERSE

The furthest stars recede
Faster than the earth moves,
Almost as fast as light;
The infinite
Adjusts itself to our need.

For far beyond the furthest, where
Light is snatched backward, no
Star leaves echo or shadow
To prove it has ever been there.

And if the universe
Reversed and showed
The colour of its money;
If now unobservable light
Flowed inward, and the skies snowed
A blizzard of galaxies,

The lens of night would burn
Brighter than the focused sun,
And man turn blinded
With white-hot darkness in his eyes.

GATHERING STICKS ON SUNDAY

If the man in the moon
Gazing at the waning earth, watches
How the frayed edge of the sunset catches
Thimbles and nodules of rock,
Hachuring distinct with threads of shadow
All that is hammered flat in the earth's brass noon;
And if he sees,
New in the level light, like pock-
marks on a face, dark craters,
The size of acorn cups, or scars
Vast as his own dried oceans, then
He'll know that soon
The living world of men
Will take a lunar look, as dead as slag,
And moon and earth will stare at one another
Like the cold, yellow skulls of child and mother.

FOR THE NEW YEAR

The stars wheel past the windows
Like flocks of winter sparrows;
The bell clangs out the hours,
And frost sparkles like stars,
And the wind blows up the dawn
With spring behind it and rain
And the spikes of daffodils
And June on fire in the hills.
The apples crowd the bough
Beneath the frosty Plough,
And autumn snow is blown
White as a harvest moon
On currant and raspberry cane,
And the wild ganders fly
Nightly across the sky.
The seasons flit like linnets,

And years whirl past like planets,
And the earth's orbit mars
The changeless map of stars.
The splintered light which now
Gently probes my eye
Is of a star that burned
When the Scots fired the land,
When the Norsemen robbed the dales
And hacked their names on the fells,
Or when the iceberg lakes
Elbowed among the rocks
And carried the Devil's stone
To the hill above the town,
Where through my dormer bay
Drizzles the Milky Way.

CLEATOR MOOR

From one shaft at Cleator Moor
They mined for coal and iron ore.
This harvest below ground could show
Black and red currants on one tree.

In furnaces they burnt the coal,
The ore was smelted into steel,
And railway lines from end to end
Corseted the bulging land.

Pylons sprouted on the fells,
Stakes were driven in like nails,
And the ploughed fields of Devonshire
Were sliced with the steel of Cleator Moor.

The land waxed fat and greedy too,
It would not share the fruits it grew,
And coal and ore, as sloe and plum,
Lay black and red for jamming time.

The pylons rusted on the fells,
The gutters leaked beside the walls,
And women searched the ebb-tide tracks
For knobs of coal or broken sticks.

But now the pits are wick with men,
Digging like dogs dig for a bone:
For food and life *we* dig the earth—
In Cleator Moor they dig for death.

Every waggon of cold coal
Is fire to drive a turbine wheel;
Every knuckle of soft ore
A bullet in a soldier's ear.

The miner at the rockface stands,
With his segged and bleeding hands
Heaps on his head the fiery coal,
And feels the iron in his soul.

BOND STREET

'Bond Street,' I said, 'Now where the devil's that?'—
The name like one whose face has been forgotten.—
He watched me from a proud-as-Preston hat;
His brief case fat with business. 'See, it's written
First on my list. Don't you know your own town?'—
'Bond Street?'—A still-born child grabbing the game
From its live-born, dying brothers.—'I copied it down
From a map in the Reading Room. In the meantime
I've a policy here—.'—Yes, on a map
Bond Street once looked the first of streets, more
Rakish than the Prince of Wales, the peak of the cap
Jaunted at then ungathered orchards of ore,
Damsons of haematite. Yet not a house
Was built there and the road remained unmade,
For there was none to pay the rates—a mouse
And whippet thoroughfare, engineered in mud,
Flagged with the green-slab leaves of dock and plantain,
A free run for the milk cart to turn round
From either of the two back-alleys shunted
End-on against it. But the birds soon found
Sites where the Council couldn't. From last year's
                                    broccoli and old
Brass bedsteads joggled in to make a fence,
Among the pigeon lofts and hen-huts, in the cold,
Green-as-a-goosegog twilight, the throstles sense
That here is the one street in all the town

That no one ever died in, that never failed
Its name or promise. The iron dust blows brown.
I turned to my enquirer.—'Bond Street I know well.
You'll sell no insurance there.'—'I could insure
The deaf and dumb,' he replied, 'against careless talk.'—
'Whatever you choose,' I said. 'A mile past the Square,
Then ask again. Hope you enjoy your walk.'

SOUTH CUMBERLAND, 10th MAY 1943

The fat flakes fall
In parachute invasion from the yellow sky.
The streets are quiet and surprised; the snow
Clutters the roofs with a wet crust, but no
Dry harbour is found on soil or wall.

In the town
The fledgling sparrows are puzzled and take fright;
The weedy hair of the slagbank in an hour turns white.
Flakes fill the tulips in backyard plots;
The chimneys snow upward and the snow smokes down.

Beyond the fells
Dawn lumbers up, and the peaks are white through the mist.
The young bracken is buttoned with snow, the knobs
Of crabapple trees are in bloom again, and blobs
Hang on the nettles like Canterbury bells.

This job is mine
And everyone's: to force our blood into the bitter day.
The hawthorn scorched and blasted by the flames of the wind
On the sheltered side greens out a dogged spray—
And this is our example, our duty and our sign.

SOUTH CUMBERLAND, 16th MAY 1943

The sun has set
Behind Black Combe, and the lower hills,
But northward in the sky the fells
Like gilded galleons on a sea of shadow
Float sunlit yet.

The liquid light
Soaks into the dry motes of the air,
Bright and moist until the flood of dawn;
Shoals of swifts round the market tower
Swim with fish-like flight.

Six days ago
The fells were limed with snow; the starlings on
        the chimney pots
Shook the falling flakes off their tin feathers.
May gives a sample of four seasons' weathers
For a week on show.

FIVE MINUTES

'I'm having five minutes,' he said,
Fitting the shelter of the cobble wall
Over his shoulders like a cape. His head
Was wrapped in a cap as green
As the lichened stone he sat on. The winter wind
Whined in the ashes like a saw,
And thorn and briar shook their red
Badges of hip and haw;
The fields were white with smoke of blowing lime;
Rusty iron brackets of sorrel stood
In grass grey as the whiskers round an old dog's nose.
'Just five minutes,' he said;
And the next day I heard that he was dead,
Having five minutes to the end of time.

OLD MAN AT A CRICKET MATCH

'It's mending worse,' he said,
    Turning west his head,
Strands of anxiety ravelled like old rope,
    Skitter of rain on the scorer's shed
        His only hope.

Seven down for forty-five,
    Catches like stings from a hive,
And every man on the boundary appealing—
    And evening when it's bad to be alive,
        And the swifts squealing.

Yet without boo or curse
He waits leg-break or hearse,
Obedient in each to lease and letter
Life and the weather mending worse,
Or worsening better.

MICHAELMAS

Like a hound with nose to the trail
The 'bus follows the road;
The road leaps up the hill.
In the valley the railway line is carved like a groove in wood;
The little towns smoke in the hollows;
The slagbanks are grey beneath the brown, bludgeoning fell.

This is the day the air has eyes,
And the Devil falls like hail
From the bright and thundering skies,
And soaks into soil and rock,
And the bad blood rises in nettle and dock,
And toadstools burst like boils between the toes of the trees.

The war that began in heaven still goes on.
Thorn trees twist like spears,
The owl haunts the grain,
The coursed rabbit weeps icicles of tears;
But the feathers of the clouds foretell
St. Michael's victory in the purged and praising rain.

THE POT GERANIUM

Green slated gables clasp the stem of the hill
In the lemony autumn sun; an acid wind
Dissolves the leaf-stalks of back-garden trees,
And chimneys with their fires unlit
Seem yet to puff a yellow smoke of poplars.
Freestone is brown as bark, and the model bakery
That once was a Primitive Methodist Chapel
Lifts its cornice against the sky.
And now, like a flight of racing pigeons
Slipped from their basket in the station yard,
A box-kite rides the air, a square of calico,
Crimson as the cornets of the Royal Temperance Band

When they brass up the wind in marching. The kite
Strains and struggles on its leash, and unseen boys,
In chicken run or allotment or by the side
Of the old quarry full to the gullet with water,
Pay out on their string a rag of dream,
High as the Jubilee flagpole.
                                    I turn from the window
(Letting the bobbins of autumn wind up the swallows)
And lie on my bed. The ceiling
Slopes over like a tent, and white walls
Wrap themselves round me, leaving only
A flap for the light to blow through. Thighs and spine
Are clamped to the mattress and looping springs
Twine round my chest and hold me. I feel the air
Move on my face like spiders, see the light
Slide across the plaster; but wind and sun
Are mine no longer, nor have I kite to claim them,
Or string to fish the clouds. But there on a shelf
In the warm corner of my dormer window
A pot geranium flies its bright balloon,
Nor can the festering hot-house of the tropics
Breed a tenser crimson, for this crock of soil,
Six inches deep by four across,
Contains the pattern, the prod and pulse of life,
Complete as the Nile or the Niger.
                                    And what need therefore
To stretch for the straining kite?—for kite and flower
Bloom in my room for ever; the light that lifts them
Shines in my own eyes, and my body's warmth
Hatches their red in my veins. It is the Gulf Stream
That rains down the chimney, making the soot spit; it is the
      Trade Wind
That blows in the draught under the bedroom door.
My ways are circumscribed, confined as a limpet
To one small radius of rock; yet
I eat the equator, breathe the sky, and carry
The great white sun in the dirt of my finger-nails.

THE CROCUS

The winter night is round me like a skull,
Hollow and black, and time has rotted off;
The sky is void, the starry creeds are null,
And death is at the throat in a soft cough.

And rooted in the leaf-mould of the brain,
I see the crocus burn, sudden as spring,
Yet not of seasons, not of sun or rain,
Bright as a ghost in the skull's scaffolding.

It is not hope, this flower, nor love its light.
It makes the darkness glow, the silence chime;
Its life gives sense to death, names black with white—
The timeless flame that is the wick of time.

AUGUST

Here the tide of summer thrusts its last
Wave, and ebbs, and leaves the white foam stranded
Among the weeds and wagons—white flowers of foam,
Wild carrot and mayweed. The sandstone wall
Dribbles with hanging plants, and the slant of the embankment
Is tousled and tussocked with grass. Up tall
Turrets of sorrel the bindweed climbs
Like a spiral staircase, and cinders from the railway
Drift in the one white bell that swings from the top.
Bramble claws among the sleepers, and its ruff of petals
Slips from the green berry, and grass and flower and weed,
Topheavy now with seed, are tired and bent.
The fists of the blooms unclinch and let the fruit
Fall from the palm of the hand. And we, in a season of work,
Close our eyes, nor count the crown of our labours,
But wait while dark pods form in the brain,
And fingers ripen in the drowse of autumn.

INNOCENTS' DAY

And Herod said: 'Sup-
posing you had been in my shoes, what would you have
Done different?—I was not thinking of myself. This
Child—whichever number might have come from the hat—could
Scarcely have begun to make trouble for twenty or
Thirty years at least, and by that time
Ten to one I'd be dead and gone. What
Matters is to keep a straight succession none can
Argue about—someone acceptable to the occupying
Power, who nevertheless will enable us to pre-
serve our sense of being a nation,

Belonging and bound to one particular place.
I know my people. They are nomads, only
Squatters here as yet. They have never left the
Wilderness. Wherever in Asia Minor the grass
Seams a dune, or a well greens a wadi, or
Sheep can feed long enough for a tent to be pitched,
There they call home, praying for daily
Manna and a nightly pillar of fire. They are
Chronic exiles; their most-sung psalms look
Back to the time of looking back. They never see
Jerusalem in the here and now, but always long to
Be where they've never been that they may long to
Be where they really are.

                                If this child had
Lived, they'd have started the same blind trek, prospecting
In sand for their own footsteps, Yes,
Mothers are weeping in the streets of Judaea, but still the
Streets are there to weep in. If that child had lived,
Not a stone would have stayed on a stone, nor a brother with
      brother,
Nor would all the Babylons of all the world
Have had water enough to swill away their tears.

                                       That
I have put a stop to, at the price
Of a two-year crop of children, making
What future observers will undoubtedly judge a
Good bargain with history.

WINDSCALE

The toadstool towers infest the shore:
Stink-horns that propagate and spore
    Wherever the wind blows.
Scafell looks down from the bracken band,
And sees hell in a grain of sand,
    And feels the canker itch between his toes.

This is a land where dirt is clean,
And poison pasture, quick and green,
    And storm sky, bright and bare;
Where sewers flow with milk, and meat
Is carved up for the fire to eat,
    And children suffocate in God's fresh air.

Alan Ross

Introduction

Alan Ross, who was born in Calcutta in 1922, was educated at Haileybury and St John's College, Oxford. During the war he served in the Royal Navy, and was mainly engaged in convoy work in destroyers based in Iceland and Russia. Included in this selection are poems from his book *Something of the Sea: Poems 1942–52* which deal with his experiences at sea. 'Survivors' has 'that casual, perhaps carefully casual, attitude towards the horrors of war which we accept today as the normal reaction. The poetry of the Second World War was emphatically not—as it was for Owen and Sassoon—in "the pity": that generalised indignation, which arose out of the intolerableness of a static front, was dissipated for Mr Ross and his fellow poets in a hundred oblique and curiously observed particularities. He writes admirably of the momentary "otherness" of those saved from death in the sea:

> Taken on board as many as lived, who
> Had a mind left for living and the ocean,
> They open eyes running with surf,
> Heavy with the grey ghosts of explosion.
>
> The meaning is not yet clear,
> Where daybreak died in the smile—
> And the mouth remained stiff
> And grinning, stupid for a little while.'

Mr Ross has said 'up to a point, poems are accidents of time and place. To say this, is to mean nothing more arbitrary or portentous than that where one happens to be conditions what one writes.' Many of his poems show his 'appreciation of place' and his ability to describe it. He has travelled widely and has written many travel books, while many of his experiences abroad are recalled in poems— 'Algerian Refugee Camp', 'Bantu on a Bicycle', and 'Grand Canal'. Among his many interests is sport. He writes: 'I have always been interested in sport, and cricket and soccer have given me as much pleasure as anything in my life.' 'Cricket at Brighton' is full of nostalgic reminiscences of Brighton before 1939, occasioned by his recollections of the Sussex *v.* Lancashire match:

> At night the Front like coloured barley-sugar; but now
> Soft blue, all soda, the air goes flat over flower-beds,
> Blue railings and beaches; below, half-painted boats, bow
> Up, settle in sand, names like Moss-Rose and Dolphin
> Drying in a breeze that flicks at the ribs of the tide.
> The chalk coastline folds up its wings of Beachy Head.
> And Worthing, fluttering white over water like brides.
> Regency squares, the Pavilion, oysters and mussels and gin.
>
> Piers like wading confectionery, esplanades of striped tulip.
> Cricket began here yesterday, the air heavy, suitable
> For medium-paced bowlers; but deck-chairs mostly were vacant,
> Faces white over startling green. Later, trains will decant
> People with baskets, litter and opinions, the seaside's staple
> Ingredients. Today Langridge pushes the ball for unfussed
> Singles; ladies clap from check rugs, talk to retired colonels:
> On tomato-red verandas the scoring rate is discussed.

NIGHT PATROL

We sail at dusk. The red moon,
Rising in a paper lantern, sets fire
To the water; the black headland disappears,
Sullen in shadow, clenched like a paw.

The docks grow flat, rubbered with mist.
Cranes, like tall drunks, hang
Over the railway. The unloading of coal
Continues under blue arc-lights.

Turning south, the moon like a rouged face
Between masts, the knotted aerials swing
Taut against the horizon, the bag
Of sea crumpled in the spray-flecked blackness.

Towards midnight the cold stars, high
Over Europe, freeze on the sky,
Stigmata above the flickering lights
Of Holland. Flashes of gunfire

Lick out over meditative coastlines, betraying
The stillness. Taking up position, night falls
Exhausted about us. The wakes
Of gunboats sew the green dark with speed.

From Dunkirk red flames open fanwise
In spokes of light; like the rising moon
Setting fire to the sky, the remote
Image of death burns on the water.

The slow muffle of hours. Clouds grow visible.
Altering course the moon congeals on a new
Bearing. Northwards again, and Europe recedes
With the first sharp splinters of dawn.

The orange sky lies over the harbour,
Derricks and pylons like scarecrows
Black in the early light. And minesweepers
Pass us, moving out slowly to the North Sea.

SURVIVORS

With the ship burning in their eyes
The white faces float like refuse
In the darkness—the water screwing
Oily circles where the hot steel lies.

They clutch with fingers frozen into claws
The lifebelts thrown from a destroyer,
And see, between the future's doors,
The gasping entrance of the sea.

Taken on board as many as lived, who
Had a mind left for living and the ocean,
They open eyes running with surf,
Heavy with the grey ghosts of explosion.

The meaning is not yet clear,
Where daybreak died in the smile—
And the mouth remained stiff
And grinning, stupid for a little while.

But soon they joke, easy and warm,
As men will who have died once
Yet somehow were able to find their way—
Muttering this was not included in their pay.

Later, sleepless at night, the brain spinning
With cracked images, they won't forget
The confusion and the oily dead,
Nor yet the casual knack of living.

ICELAND IN WARTIME

Green and red lights flank the inlet mouth,
As it were a night-club. But three days south,
Below grey Scottish hills, I read a book
About this island, arranged mentally its outward look,
Catalogued its properties: sulphur, sagas, geysers
And sphagnum moss; rocks rising in snow-ribbed tiers
Over fiords. A slate sky. But now we have arrived
By night, lucky and thankful to have survived,
I was not ready for this blaze of light,

A shield over the harbour, nor the moon like a kite
Tying its lemon rays to the muzzled mountains,
Laying out for inspection what the bay contains:
Destroyers, sweepers, oilers and corvettes.
And there, coming to greet us, the silhouettes
Of launches, their wakes throwing up phosphorus
Like a northern champagne. They'll have sailing orders for us:
And before even checking what I imagine
Dawn here to look like, spilling over the snowline
And bald rock the crimson canister of the sun,
We shall be off, the convoy behind us in echelon.

CRICKET AT BRIGHTON

At night the Front like coloured barley-sugar; but now
Soft blue, all soda, the air goes flat over flower-beds,
Blue railings and beaches; below, half-painted boats, bow
Up, settle in sand, names like Moss-Rose and Dolphin
Drying in a breeze that flicks at the ribs of the tide.
The chalk coastline folds up its wings of Beachy Head
And Worthing, fluttering white over water like brides.
Regency squares, the Pavilion, oysters and mussels and gin.

Piers like wading confectionery, esplanades of striped tulip.
Cricket began here yesterday, the air heavy, suitable
For medium-paced bowlers; but deck-chairs mostly were vacant,
Faces white over startling green. Later, trains will decant
People with baskets, litter and opinions, the seaside's staple
Ingredients. Today Langridge pushes the ball for unfussed
Singles; ladies clap from check rugs, talk to retired colonels:
On tomato-red verandas the scoring rate is discussed.

Sussex v. Lancashire, the air birded and green after rain,
Dew on syringa and cherry. Seaward the water
Is satin, pale emerald, fretted with lace at the edges,
The whole sky rinsed easy like nerves after pain.
May here is childhood, lost somewhere between and never
Recovered, but again moved nearer, as a lever
Turned on the pier flickers the past into pictures.
A time of immediacy, optimism, without stricture.

Postcards and bathing-machines and old prints.
Something comes back, the inkling, the momentary hint
Of what we had wanted to be, though differently now,

For the conditions are different and what we had wanted
We wanted as we were then, without conscience, unhaunted,
And given the chance must refuse to want it again.
Only, occasionally, we escape, we return where we were:
Watching cricket at Brighton, Cornford bowling through
      sea-scented air.

WINTER BOATS AT BRIGHTON

They huddle in groups on shingle, aiming
Bows bearing loved names—Tiger, Seashell, Deirdre,
The Fifteen-Two—where painted ironwork flakes
Over them, lack of light maiming

The whole coastline, passive under seas creaming
Mauve-green. Seaweed, like ribbons streaming from hats
Worn by girls in pictures by Berthe Morisot,
Criss-crosses the beach, emptily dreaming—

And the boats, paired for comfort, sad shapes
Beneath dwindled tamarisk, wear salt
Along gunwales, thin white coverings like capes
Drawn in a taut line from stern to stem.

Gulls screech from domes of pier, from Pavilion cupolas,
To snatch wet bread flung by blue-jerseyed men,
Braced against breezes, making small steps
By their boats, ten paces eastward, then west ten—

The names a kind of mnemonic, Deirdre, Seashell,
Maria—waiting to reinhabit them, to come alive,
—Boats, men, at a standstill—for summer to dive
On them with love, with promise of the sea-swell.

NORTH LONDON

Beyond the window, the tyre-coloured road deflates
Like a tube at night; the load of the day—
Red-stuccoed houses, a Victorian baroque that dates
The whole hill with its ugliness, the bay
Windows of dentists, landladies and veterinary surgeons—
Subsides on the tarmac, the trees dusted with white,
And from the huge blocks of flats

People emerge, testing the evening, smelling for the first
Time air, leaves, the flowers that lean on the light.

A ritual almost, this dog-like smelling with enquiring
Noses, cleared of rubber, smoke-stacks and gas;
The walk with wife or pet, continents clearing
Their guilt behind enormous spectacles, a mass
Of words clumsily analysing what everyone is fearing.
Yet, for us as much as for any, this dead-end
Of the day, the air rinsed, lends its magic
To our feelings, and what tends
To remain with us is a sense
Of proportion, a sentimentalising of the inherent
Boredom of cities, into the miraculous, the tragic—

A state where anything might happen, the identity
Between what is important and what we may
Become suddenly established—each new day
Something to greet with alacrity—
And even the limits of this temporary horizon,
A grey hill of shops and flats, restaurants
And villas tempered with limes, does not oppress;
For in the hazy, window-lit valley
Below us, move images our writing fingers may sometimes
        undress.

EMBANKMENT BEFORE SNOW

A zinc afternoon. The barges black,
And black the funnels of tugs nosing
Phlegm-coloured waves slap slapping
Stone wharves. A smell of sacking
And soot. Grey chimneys and statues
Grey with cold, and grey life-belts.
                    Now the arthritic gulls,
Seedy with displeasure, crotchet on railings,
Falling with a flat splash on wet bread.
Green is under black in the gardens
Bearing the frozen face of Huskisson,
Statesman, but trees are black all through.
The sun fumes behind mist which rises
To thicken this smoke, make dusk black.
The river, eyed by launches, hangs its cranes
                    To grab nothing
But cold black air aqueous and rotting.

ROCK PAINTINGS, DRAKENSBERG

These mountains of up-pointed spears
Hold eland, oribi and rhebok
Capering over yellow rock
To sandstone caves that form a barrier

Eastward mauve and vertical,
Westward greenly gradual.
Sweet grasses swish below like silk
Torn at dark by prowling buck.

Baboons on red and scrabbling paths
Scatter dust in layers of talc,
Imitating as they stalk
Human gestures, hurling oaths.

A form of sympathetic magic
More goodnatured now than tragic,
Though practised by the bushman hunter,
Re-creating as a painter

Animals he hoped to capture,
Art was not a surplus rapture,
But a means of softening up
Hartebeest and antelope.

Here walls of cave and sky converge;
Within, the human primal urge.
Brush-pigs scuttle from cracked rocks,
Bush-girls thrust their weighted buttocks

Squatting as they chant in line
Round pots of boiling porcupine.
The painted bushman aims his bow,
The real sunset starts to flow

Across this sweeping mountain range
And still, despite ten centuries' change,
Art remains a kind of hunt
Eliminating fear and cant,

A means of pinning down
An object, by the sheer act
Of drawing animal or loved one,
Making absence into fact.

You have black eyes,
Four years of age,
A chic, cast-off coat
—pepper-and-salt, double-breasted,
A label naming you 'Mohammed',
Some slippers, a squashed felt hat.
Nothing else. And 'nothing' means just that.

This camp is your home until—well, until.
A flag flaps on a hill.
The *oued* soon will be dry;
Do you know how to cry?

Smoke curls from the tents
Where women who are not your mother,
Hennaed and trinketed, cook.
Your eyes see but do not look.
And men who are not your father,
Turbaned and burned, sit stiff
In rows, like clay pigeons, on a cliff.
Targets do not easily relax.
Your hair is fair as flax.

Guns rattle the mauve hills
Where the last warmth spills
On villages where once you were
One of a family that died.
Not much else. Just that.

You pull down the brim of your hat.
I do not know what goes on inside.

BANTU ON A BICYCLE

This Bantu on a bicycle racing the sunset
Carries on his shoulder, like a rifle
At the slope, a torn umbrella that
Would pass no sergeant. He will get wet
Anyway, or, if storms fail, will stifle,
For townships are hot. But, unfurled,
His gamp waves like a shield, his hat
Squashes his ears and, sodden, his vest

Takes like a transfer the sunset's medals,
Saffron and crimson. The last burst now, he pedals
As if announcing the end of the world,
Which event alone might curb his unrest.

NELSON AT PALERMO

Monte Pellegrino, mauve, bald and granite skull
That holds Palermo in vast dull
Shade, entrapped the languors and the heat
Of summer in the golden shell whose neat
Cubed villas lay where waters lapped
The Porta Felice and its trapped
And groaning court; the Bourbon King and Queen,
Sir William H., rickety Pantaloon,
And Nelson, Harlequin to Columbine.
The *coup de foudre* can strike at any time,
It seems; one-armed, one-eyed and 39
Years aged with fevers, ague and wounds
He felt himself a fox pursued by hounds,
Courtiers, lazzarini, C-in-C's. Before the kill,
Though, in his arm the beloved vixen lay.

A sailor lives by names: the Nile, Aboukir Bay,
Boreas, Vanguard, Foudroyant, and here,
Inactive at a foreign court, the one
Most potent of them all, 'dear Lady Hamilton',
Become, by stages now impenetrable, 'my love',
'My darling angel'. 'Ever for ever, I am yours,
Only yours, Even beyond this world'. The one
Word *Emma* joins the names of ships,
The buoyant prow attached to dazzling lips.

Fireworks at La Favorita, *fêtes champêtres*,
Hard gales, and after supper at La Nova,
Faro into the dawn. The non-playing hero fell asleep,
The look of love a film across the eyes.
The day began at five. No wonder Orpheus nods.
Cards are for ambassadresses, not for gods.

Palm-trees, oranges, ochre and grey pavilions,
Ennui sustained by passion. Emma bloomed.
Together, in small tavernas, side by side

They watched the drunken sailors reel on board,
'Viva Nelson' the cry when they were recognised.
At Palazzo Palagonia champagne flowed,
Night after night: revolution here was stayed,

With public hangings watched by thronging crowds.
Nelson might fidget, hate the climate
And that illiberal bore, the Queen, but she
Was antidote to civil servants, frets, the rain:
The noose of thraldom stronger than the pain
Of having to choose, of making his interest plain.

AGRIGENTO

Temples, yes, there are temples, dung-coloured,
Coarse, but numerous, sweeping the plain
At level intervals. Doric and civicly decent,
Though to my eye dull. Nevertheless, more
Of Akragas is here than of most Greek cities.
It would be ungracious not to admit it.
How, then, account for the disappointment,
The feeling that whatever was here is spent,
And this ugly town sprawling an escarpment
Merely gratuitous? Our several pities
Might be devoted to its unshaven inhabitants
Hangdog somewhat, with the miserly resentment
Of those observing their rightful patrimony
Squandered each year. To live thus,
In the shadow of history, the city
Once famous for horses, chariots, winners
Of Olympics, a mere adjunct of factories
And quarries, something for tourists to gape at,
Cannot be good for the expression; Empedocles,
Acron, they had better value, though the view
From a distance, of stubble, blueness and sea
Scarcely has altered, and even Pirandello,
Chasing his tail here, rarely complained.
Still, the run-down feeling persists, we are glad
To shake off the dust of these dusty emplacements,
Before cafard sets in, and we start counting
The cobwebs, noting the bare sockets of bulbs,
The stinking lavatories, the gloomy hotel
Where nothing pulls, neither chain nor bell,
We are free as air, and it's just as well.

GRAND CANAL

Your hair that makes the most of vines,
Blue shirt against the trellis, and goggles
Like insect's eyes, reflecting the lagoon.

That's all the Kodacolour yields
To which I add a table
Where Negronis glint, a liquid air

That melts between view-finder and the view.
The lap of gondolas, of subdued jazz,
Great domes that squeeze the sun,

The biscuit palaces, exist without,
Beyond the edges of the fading print.
It was a time of meeting elsewhere soon,

Of brief goodbyes in golden afternoon.
I look again and feel the first
Faint smears of rust in autumn's deadly tune.

WINTER GULLS

Treetops, spires and houses—all have grown
Plumper under overcoats of snow: a rubber-coloured morning
Where square-gardens are knee-deep in silence. Everything
Is muffled but solid: a district of respectable footsteps.
Now the albino sun lights in some crows
That claw stiffly at branches with talons like forceps.

Suddenly, to patches of slate visible like baldness
Under snow, a scurry of gulls comes wheeling white
Past the window. The snow where they vainly grip
Flurries into air, a waste-paper world that slips.
What was reassuring before now seems aimless and light,
And the whole skyline unreliable, skittish as a kite.

Soon it recovers, and a hypocrite air descends
That tries to persuade us that life is just as before.
But now we know different—for the gulls,
Startled, gave us the tip that nothing
In quite the same way will be ever secure—
For us, fated to drift on a glitter that dulls;
Like them, effigies stuffed on painted and scented hulls.

R. S. Thomas

(The following is reprinted by permission from an article by Benedict Nightingale in *The Guardian.*)

The characteristic conflict of R. S. Thomas's poetry is between the instinctual life of the Welsh peasant, rooted deep in the earth, and the menaces of civilisation; the creep of industrialism, the spread of the English way of life, the sterilising intellectualisation of living. From the conflict emerges a powerfully felt, rather Yeatsian philosophy that grips and challenges; and it is, indeed, for their lack of comprehensive philosophy that R. S. Thomas criticises his contemporaries.

Before moving to Eglwysfach, R. S. Thomas was rector of Manafon, an isolated agricultural parish near Newtown, and here he found Prytherch and the other Thomas peasants—'tough, hard narrow men'. Their way of life exhilarated him, but he knows it is disappearing, and this saddens him. He thinks the importance of science and technology overrated; they bring as many problems as benefits: he sees, indeed, the Industrial Revolution as the beginning of the end for Wales. 'People tell me I couldn't do without a motor car, but of course I could. It isn't necessary.' He resents, particularly, the teeming holidaymakers whose cars invade the peace of the road outside his home in the summer months. He is proud of the Celt in him, and declares himself sympathetic with the Welsh nationalists. He would like to see Wales economically and politically independent of England. English dam projects and reservoirs disturb him; and so does the flood of English coming to settle in Wales—'every new Englishman is another nail in the coffin of Wales'. The trouble is, he says, that the Welsh welcome newcomers; perhaps they are too open-handed. He admits to a dislike of the English proletariat, of the English upper classes, and of the cold respectability of the middle classes; but is prepared to like the intelligent Englishman as long as he doesn't try to impose his way of life. He shudders from the spread of urbanisation, and says he never willingly goes near a town; London is the best of a bad lot. R. S. Thomas clings to an ideal of simple living, and is willing to admit himself irrational in some of his attitudes.

'But they are all one has to fall back on. One knows it is all rather hopeless, but one feels it all the same. Reason may say that science and progress are valuable—they relieve hunger, and so on—yet one's feelings, the poetry in one, seem to say something quite different, beyond reason.'

He finds that life as a pastor, though it is more taxing than many think, leaves him plenty of time to write. In general the poems he considers best come to him quickly; if he has to fight for words they tend to be less successful. He never rewrites once a poem is completed. He may spend a whole day at his desk toying with an idea for a lyric and find himself with nothing except the practice and experience of trying: 'One is like a fisherman playing a fish, getting the sense of it.' The image is characteristic; his poetry is a shoal of metaphors from the woods and the hills, and he seems to be surprised to be asked if they come easily to him: they evidently do.

TOO LATE

I would have spared you this, Prytherch;
You were like a child to me.
I would have seen you poor and in rags,
Rather than wealthy and not free.

The rain and wind are hard masters;
I have known you wince under their lash.
But there was comfort for you at the day's end
Dreaming over the warm ash

Of a turf fire on a hill farm,
Contented with your accustomed ration
Of bread and bacon, and drawing your strength
From membership of an old nation

Not given to beg. But look at yourself
Now, a servant hired to flog
The life out of the slow soil,
Or come obediently as a dog

To the pound's whistle. Can't you see
Behind the smile on the times' face
The cold brain of the machine
That will destroy you and your race?

LAMENT FOR PRYTHERCH

When I was young, when I was young!
Were you ever young, Prytherch, a rich farmer:
Cows in the byre, sheep in the pen,
A brown egg under each hen,
The barns oozing corn like honey?
You are old now; time's geometry
Upon your face by which we tell
Your sum of years has with sharp care
Conspired and crossed your brow with grief.
Your heart that is dry as a dead leaf
Undone by frost's cruel chemistry
Clings in vain to the bare bough
Where once in April a bird sang.

SERVANT

You served me well, Prytherch.
From all my questionings and doubts;
From brief acceptance of the times'
Deities; from ache of the mind
Or body's tyranny, I turned,
Often after a whole year,
Often twice in the same day,
To where you read in the slow book
Of the farm, turning the fields' pages
So patiently, never tired
Of the land's story; not just believing,
But proving in your bone and your blood
Its accuracy; willing to stand
Always aside from the main road,
Where life's flashier illustrations
Were marginal.
           Not that you gave
The whole answer. Is truth so bare,
So dark, so dumb, as on your hearth
And in your company I found it?
Is not the evolving print of the sky
To be read, too; the mineral
Of the mind worked? Is not truth choice,
With a clear eye and a free hand,
From life's bounty?
           Not choice for you,
But seed sown upon the thin
Soil of a heart, not rich, nor fertile,
Yet capable of the one crop,
Which is the bread of truth that I break.

A WELSH TESTAMENT

All right, I was Welsh. Does it matter?
I spoke the tongue that was passed on
To me in the place I happened to be,
A place huddled between grey walls
Of cloud for at least half the year.
My word for heaven was not yours.
The word for hell had a sharp edge
Put on it by the hand of the wind

Honing, honing with a shrill sound
Day and night. Nothing that Glyn Dŵr
Knew was armour against the rain's
Missiles. What was descent from him?

Even God had a Welsh name:
We spoke to him in the old language;
He was to have a peculiar care
For the Welsh people. History showed us
He was too big to be nailed to the wall
Of a stone chapel, yet still we crammed him
Between the boards of a black book.

Yet men sought us despite this.
My high cheek-bones, my length of skull
Drew them as to a rare portrait
By a dead master. I saw them stare
From their long cars, as I passed knee-deep
In ewes and wethers. I saw them stand
By the thorn hedges, watching me string
The far flocks on a shrill whistle.

And always there was their eyes' strong
Pressure on me: You are Welsh, they said;
Speak to us so; keep your fields free
Of the smell of petrol, the loud roar
Of hot tractors; we must have peace
And quietness.
                                    Is a museum
Peace? I asked. Am I the keeper
Of the heart's relics, blowing the dust
In my own eyes? I am a man;
I never wanted the drab role
Life assigned me, an actor playing
To the past's audience upon a stage
Of earth and stone; the absurd label
Of birth, of race hanging askew
About my shoulders. I was in prison
Until you came; your voice was a key
Turning in the enormous lock
Of hopelessness. Did the door open
To let me out or yourselves in?

WELSH HISTORY

We were a people taut for war; the hills
Were no harder, the thin grass
Clothed them more warmly than the coarse
Shirts our small bones.
We fought, and were always in retreat,
Like snow thawing upon the slopes
Of Mynydd Mawr; and yet the stranger
Never found our ultimate stand
In the thick woods, declaiming verse
To the sharp prompting of the harp.

Our kings died, or they were slain
By the old treachery at the ford.
Our bards perished, driven from the halls
Of nobles by the thorn and bramble.

We were a people bred on legends,
Warming our hands at the red past.
The great were ashamed of our loose rags
Clinging stubbornly to the proud tree
Of blood and birth, our lean bellies
And mud houses were a proof
Of our ineptitude for life.

We were a people wasting ourselves
In fruitless battles for our masters,
In lands to which we had no claim,
With men for whom we felt no hatred.

We were a people, and are so yet.
When we have finished quarrelling for crumbs
Under the table, or gnawing the bones
Of a dead culture, we will arise,
Armed, but not in the old way.

WELSH LANDSCAPE

To live in Wales is to be conscious
At dusk of the spilled blood
That went to the making of the wild sky,
Dyeing the immaculate rivers
In all their courses.
It is to be aware,

Above the noisy tractor
And hum of the machine
Of strife in the strung woods,
Vibrant with sped arrows.
You cannot live in the present,
At least not in Wales.
There is the language for instance,
The soft consonants
Strange to the ear.
There are cries in the dark at night
As owls answer the moon,
And thick ambush of shadows,
Hushed at the fields' corners.
There is no present in Wales,
And no future;
There is only the past,
Brittle with relics,
Wind-bitten towers and castles
With sham ghosts;
Mouldering quarries and mines;
And an impotent people,
Sick with inbreeding,
Worrying the carcase of an old song.

LOOKING AT SHEEP

Yes, I know. They are like primroses;
Their ears are the colour of the stems
Of primroses; and their eyes—
Two halves of a nut.
                              But images
Like this are for sheer fancy
To play with. Seeing how Wales fares
Now, I will attend rather
To things as they are: to green grass
That is not ours; to visitors
Buying us up. Thousands of mouths
Are emptying their waste speech
About us, and an Elsan culture
Threatens us.
                              What would they say
Who bled here, warriors
Of a free people? Savagely
On castles they were the sole cause
Of the sun still goes down red.

ON THE FARM

There was Dai Puw. He was no good.
They put him in the fields to dock swedes,
And took the knife from him, when he came home
At late evening with a grin
Like the slash of a knife on his face.

There was Llew Puw, and he was no good.
Every evening after the ploughing
With the big tractor he would sit in his chair,
And stare into the tangled fire garden,
Opening his slow lips like a snail.

There was Huw Puw, too. What shall I say?
I have heard him whistling in the hedges
On and on, as though winter
Would never again leave those fields,
And all the trees were deformed.

And lastly there was the girl:
Beauty under some spell of the beast.
Her pale face was the lantern
By which they read in life's dark book
The shrill sentence: God is love.

THE MUCK FARMER

This man swaying dully before us
Is a muck farmer, to use his own words;
A man unfit to breed the sleek herds,
That win prizes and give the thick milk,
White as the teeth it builds. His rare smile,
Cracked as the windows of his stone house
Sagging under its weight of moss,
Falls on us palely like the wan moon
That cannot pierce the thin cloud
Of March. His speech is a rank garden,
Where thought is choked in the wild tangle
Of vain phrases.
            Leave him, then, crazed and alone
To pleach his dreams with his rough hands.
Our ways have crossed and tend now apart;
Ours to end in a field wisely sown,
His in the mixen of his warped heart.

THE LABOURER

There he goes, tacking against the fields'
Uneasy tides. What have the centuries done
To change him? The same garments, frayed with light
Or seamed with rain, cling to the wind-scoured bones
And shame him in the eyes of the spruce birds.
Once it was ignorance, then need, but now
Habit that drapes him on a bush of cloud
For life to mock at, while the noisy surf
Of people dins far off at the world's rim.
He has been here since life began, a vague
Movement among the roots of the young grass.
Bend down and peer beneath the twigs of hair,
And look into the hard eyes, flecked with care;
What do you see? Notice the twitching hands,
Veined like a leaf, and tough bark of the limbs,
Wrinkled and gnarled, and tell me what you think.
A wild tree still, whose seasons are not yours,
The slow heart beating to the hidden pulse,
Of the strong sap, the feet firm in the soil?
No, no, a man like you, but blind with tears
Of sweat to the bright star that draws you on.

THE POACHER

Turning aside, never meeting
In the still lanes, fly infested,
Our frank greeting with quick smile,
You are the wind that set the bramble
Aimlessly clawing the void air.
The fox knows you, the sly weasel
Feels always the steel comb
Of eyes parting like sharp rain
Among the grasses its smooth fur.
No smoke haunting the cold chimney
Over your hearth betrays your dwelling
In blue writing above the trees.
The robed night, your dark familiar,
Covers your movements; the slick sun,
A dawn accomplice, removes your tracks
One by one from the bright dew.

AFFINITY

Consider this man in the field beneath,
Gaitered with mud, lost in his own breath,
Without joy, without sorrow,
Without children, without wife,
Stumbling insensitively from furrow to furrow,
A vague somnambulist; but hold your tears,
For his name also is written in the Book of Life.

Ransack your brainbox, pull out the drawers
That rot in your heart's dust, and what have you to give
To enrich his spirit or the way he lives?
From the standpoint of education or caste or creed
Is there anything to show that your essential need
Is less than his, who has the world for church,
And stands bare-headed in the woods' wide porch
Morning and evening to hear God's choir
Scatter their praises? Don't be taken in
By stinking garments or an aimless grin;
He also is human, and the same small star,
That lights you homeward, has inflamed his mind
With the old hunger, born of his kind.

AUTUMN ON THE LAND

A man, a field, silence—what is there to say?
He lives, he moves, and the October day
Burns slowly down.
               History is made
Elsewhere; the hours forfeit to time's blade
Don't matter here. The leaves large and small,
Shed by the branches, unlamented fall
About his shoulders. You may look in vain
Through the eyes' window; on his meagre hearth
The thin, shy soul has not begun its reign
Over the darkness. Beauty, love and mirth
And joy are strangers there.
                    You must revise
Your bland philosophy of nature, earth
Has of itself no power to make men wise.

THE VIEW FROM THE WINDOW

Like a painting it is set before one,
But less brittle, ageless; these colours
Are renewed daily with variations
Of light and distance that no painter
Achieves or suggests. Then there is movement,
Change, as slowly the cloud bruises
Are healed by sunlight, or snow caps
A black mood; but gold at evening
To cheer the heart. All through history
The great brush has not rested,
Nor the paint dried; yet what eye,
Looking coolly, or, as we now,
Through the tears' lenses, ever saw
This work and it was not finished?

A BLACKBIRD SINGING

It seems wrong that out of this bird,
Black, bold, a suggestion of dark
Places about it, there yet should come
Such rich music, as though the notes'
Ore were changed to a rare metal
At one touch of that bright bill.

You have heard it often, alone at your desk
In a green April, your mind drawn
Away from its work by sweet disturbance
Of the mild evening outside your room.

A slow singer, but loading each phrase
With history's overtones, love, joy
And grief learned by his dark tribe
In other orchards and passed on
Instinctively as they are now,
But fresh always with new tears.

PISCES

Who said to the trout,
You shall die on Good Friday
To be food for a man
And his pretty lady?

It was I, said God,
Who formed the roses
In the delicate flesh
And the tooth that bruises.

POETRY FOR SUPPER

'Listen, now, verse should be as natural
As the small tuber that feeds on muck
And grows slowly from obtuse soil
To the white flower of immortal beauty.'

'Natural, hell! What was it Chaucer
Said once about the long toil
That goes like blood to the poem's making?
Leave it to nature and the verse sprawls,
Limp as bindweed, if it break at all
Life's iron crust. Man, you must sweat
And rhyme your guts taut, if you'd build
Your verse a ladder.'
                        'You speak as though
No sunlight ever surprised the mind
Groping on its cloudy path.'

'Sunlight's a thing that needs a window
Before it enter a dark room.
Windows don't happen.'
                        So two old poets,
Hunched at their beer in the low haze
Of an inn parlour, while the talk ran
Noisily by them, glib with prose.

Sources and Acknowledgments

Thanks are due to the authors, their representatives and publishers mentioned in the following list for their kind permission to reproduce copyright material:

John Betjeman: 'Upper Lambourne', 'Greenaway', 'Bristol and Clifton', 'In Westminster Abbey', 'Sunday Morning, King's Cambridge', 'The Village Inn', 'Diary of a Church Mouse', 'Christmas', from *Collected Poems* (John Murray Ltd); 'London' from *Summoned by Bells* (John Murray Ltd).

Charles Causley: 'King's College Chapel', 'The Seasons in North Cornwall', 'Keats at Teignmouth', 'Song of the Dying Gunner A.A.1.', 'Chief Petty Officer', 'Convoy', 'At the British War Cemetery, Bayeux', 'Death of an Aircraft', 'Cowboy Song', 'My Friend Maloney', 'Nursery Rhyme of Innocence and Experience', from *Union Street* (Rupert Hart-Davis Ltd); 'Innocent's Song', 'At Grantchester', 'For an Ex-Far East Prisoner of War', 'A Ballad of Charlotte Dymond', from *Johnny Alleluia* (Rupert Hart-Davis Ltd).

Patric Dickinson: 'Jodrell Bank', 'On Dow Crag', 'Bluebells', 'The Redwing', 'The Roman Wall', from *The World I See* (Chatto and Windus Ltd); 'The Scale of Things', 'Heartbreak House', 'Lines for an Eminent Poet and Critic', 'Geologic', from *The Scale of Things* (Chatto and Windus Ltd); 'Common Terns', 'The Royal Military Canal', 'Lament for the Great Yachts', from *The Sailing Race* (Chatto and Windus Ltd); 'The Onset' from *Theseus and the Minotaur* (Jonathan Cape Ltd); 'The Dam' from *The Stone in the Midst* (Methuen and Co. Ltd).

Clifford Dyment: 'The Axe in the Wood', 'Holidays in Childhood', 'Coming of the Fog', from *The Axe in the Wood* (J. M. Dent and Sons Ltd); 'The Winter Trees', 'Carrion', 'Man and Beast', ' "From Many a Mangled Truth a War is Won" ', 'Fox', 'A Switch Cut in April', 'The Swans', and ' "Savage the Daylight and Annihilate Night" ', from *Poems 1935–1948* (J. M. Dent and Sons Ltd); 'The Carpenter', 'The King of the Wood', 'The Dark City', 'Bahnhofstrasse', from *Experiences and Places* (J. M. Dent and Sons Ltd); 'The Raven', 'The Desert'.

Ted Hughes: 'Bayonet Charge', 'Griefs for Dead Soldiers', 'Six Young Men', 'Roarers in a Ring', 'The Jaguar', 'The Horses', 'Song', from *The Hawk in the Rain* (Faber and Faber Ltd); 'Dick Straightup', 'Hawk

Roosting', 'Thrushes', 'Pike', 'View of a Pig', 'Esther's Tomcat', 'November', from *Lupercal* (Faber and Faber Ltd).

James Kirkup: 'The Submerged Village' from *The Submerged Village* (Oxford University Press); 'A City of the North', 'The Bowl of Goldfish: a Fable', 'A Charm for the Ear-Ache', from *A Correct Compassion* (Oxford University Press); 'A Visit to Brontëland' from *A Spring Journey* (Oxford University Press); 'Ghosts, Fire, Water', 'To the Ancestral North', 'For the 90th Birthday of Sibelius', 'To an Old Lady Asleep at a Poetry Reading', 'The Shepherd's Tale', from *The Descent into the Cave* (Oxford University Press); 'Seven Pictures from China: v Landscape and vii Autumn Grove after Rain', 'Sakunami', 'Tea in a Space-Ship', 'Earthquake', from *The Prodigal Son* (Oxford University Press); 'Rugby League Game', 'No More Hiroshimas', from *Refusal to Conform* (Oxford University Press).

Laurie Lee: 'Seafront', 'The Long War', 'The Three Winds', from *The Sun My Monument* (Chatto and Windus Ltd); 'April Rise', 'Field of Autumn', 'Christmas Landscape', from *The Bloom of Candles* (John Lehmann Ltd); 'My Many-Coated Man', 'Sunken Evening', 'Bombay Arrival', 'Scot in the Desert', 'Home from Abroad', 'Apples', 'Town Owl', from *My Many-Coated Man* (André Deutsch Ltd); 'Stork in Jerez' (Pocket Poets, Vista Books); 'Cock-Pheasant' (reproduced by courtesy of *Vogue*).

Norman Nicholson: 'For the New Year', 'Cleator Moor', 'South Cumberland, 10th May 1943', 'South Cumberland, 16th May 1943', 'Michaelmas', from *Five Rivers* (Faber and Faber Ltd); 'The Crocus', 'August', from *Rock Face* (Faber and Faber Ltd); 'The Pot Geranium', 'Gathering Sticks on Sunday', 'The Undiscovered Planet', 'The Expanding Universe', 'Five Minutes', 'Innocents' Day', from *The Pot Geranium* (Faber and Faber Ltd); 'Old Man at a Cricket Match', 'Bond Street', 'Windscale'.

Alan Ross: 'Night Patrol', 'Survivors', 'Iceland in Wartime', 'Cricket at Brighton', 'North London', 'Winter Gulls', from *Something of the Sea* (André Deutsch Ltd); 'Winter Boats at Brighton', 'Embankment before Snow', from *To Whom It May Concern* (Hamish Hamilton Ltd); 'Rock Paintings, Drakensberg', 'Algerian Refugee Camp, Aïn-Khemouda', 'Bantu on a Bicycle', from *African Negatives* (Eyre and Spottiswoode (Publishers) Ltd); 'Nelson at Palermo' (published in *The New Statesman*); 'Agrigento' (published in *The Twentieth Century*); 'Grand Canal' (published in *The Spectator*).

R. S. Thomas: 'Lament for Prytherch', 'Welsh History', 'Welsh Landscape', 'The Labourer', 'The Poacher', 'Affinity', 'Autumn on the Land', 'Pisces', from *Song at the Year's Turning* (Rupert Hart-Davis Ltd); 'The Muck Farmer', 'The View from the Window', 'A Blackbird Singing', 'Poetry for Supper', from *Poetry for Supper* (Rupert Hart-

Davis Ltd); 'Too Late', 'A Welsh Testament', from *Tares* (Rupert Hart-Davis Ltd); 'Servant', 'Looking at Sheep', 'On the Farm', from *The Bread of Truth* (Rupert Hart-Davis Ltd).

Introduction to John Betjeman's poems: extracts from *John Betjeman* by Derek Stanford (Neville Spearman Ltd). Introduction to Ted Hughes's poems: extracts from 'Ted Hughes' by A. E. Dyson (published in *The Critical Quarterly*). Introduction to R. S. Thomas's poems: excerpt from an article by Benedict Nightingale (reprinted by permission of *The Guardian*).

Index of First Lines

A man, a field, silence—what is there to say?, p. 150
A raven crouched in a tree, p. 61
A yellowhammer in her mouth, the cat came mewing, p. 58
A zinc afternoon. The barges black, p. 135
Adrift in space, p. 85
Against the evening sky the trees are black, p. 55
All day the sand, like golden chains, p. 109
All right, I was Welsh. Does it matter?, p. 144
An old man's flamingo-coloured kite, p. 90
And Herod said: 'Sup-, p. 127
At night the Front like coloured barley-sugar; but now, p. 133
At the station exit, my bundle in hand, p. 89

Bank Holiday. A sky of guns. The river, p. 21
Behold the apples' rounded worlds:, p. 113
Beside a dune high as a tree, p. 60
Beyond the window, the tyre-coloured road deflates, p. 134
'Bond Street,' I said, 'Now where the devil's that?'—, p. 122
By the wild sea-wall I wandered, p. 20

Calm, the surrounding mountains look upon, p. 91
Consider this man in the field beneath, p. 150

Daylong this tomcat lies stretched flat, p. 76
Draw the blanket of ocean, p. 24

Exploiter of the shadows, p. 54

Far-fetched with tales of other worlds and ways, p. 109
File into yellow candle light, fair choristers of King's, p. 7
From a mountainside, p. 85
From many a mangled truth a war is won, p. 57
From one shaft at Cleator Moor, p. 121
From that elemental land, p. 97

Gilded with leaf-thick paint; a steady, p. 115
Green and red lights flank the inlet mouth, p. 132
Green slated gables clasp the stem of the hill, p. 125

He has come to such a pitch, p. 46
He is older than the naval side of British history, p. 22
Here among long-discarded cassocks, p. 9
Here like the maze of our bewilderment, p. 110
Here the tide of summer thrusts its last, p. 127
Hugging the ground by the lilac tree, p. 58

I am that man with helmet made of thorn, p. 21
I climbed through woods in the hour-before-dawn dark, p. 71
I come from Salem County, p. 27
I had a silver penny, p. 29
I know so well this turfy mile, p. 3
I sit in the top of the wood, my eyes closed, p. 72
I stopped to watch a man strike at the trunk, p. 57
I walked where in their talking graves, p. 24
I was holding my son's hand, p. 39
I would have spared you this, Prytherch;, p. 143
If ever I saw blessing in the air, p. 111
If the man in the moon, p. 120
'I'm having five minutes,' he said, p. 124
In agony of mind, in the west country, p. 43
In the city of Sendai, electric cold, p. 86
In this world a tablecloth need not be laid, p. 101
It seems wrong that out of this bird, p. 151
'It's mending worse,' he said, p. 124
It was a Sunday evening, p. 31

Last year Harold was making a boat, p. 53
Less passionate the long war throws, p. 110
Let me take this other glove off, p. 6
Like a hound with nose to the trail, p. 125
Like a painting it is set before one, p. 151
Like smoke held down by frost, p. 39
'Listen now, verse should be as natural, p. 152

Midstream they met. Challenger and champion, p. 55
Mightiest, like some universal cataclysm, p. 65
Monte Pellegrino, mauve, bald and granite skull, p. 138
My friend Maloney, eighteen, p. 28

Night slides down the mountain side, p. 56
Now let music, light as an enchanter's hands, p. 103

O lady, when the tipped cup of the moon blessed you, p. 78
O spring has set off her green fuses, p. 19
Oh mother my mouth is full of stars, p. 22
On eves of cold, when slow coal fires, p. 114
One day on our village in the month of July, p. 25
Only the lamps are live, p. 56
Out of green and stony dales, where, like enormous dice, p. 95
Out on the furthest tether let it run, p. 119

Past eighty, but never in eighty years —, p. 69
Pike, three inches long, perfect, p. 74

Quiet as conscience on the Stock Exchange, p. 42

Savage the daylight and annihilate night, p. 60
Slow-hooved across the carrion sea, p. 108
Slow moves the acid breath of noon, p. 112
Snore on in your front-row chair! Let not my voice, p. 100
Snow fell as for Wenceslas, p. 68
Sport is absurd, and sad, p. 99
Suddenly he awoke and was running—raw, p. 65
Suddenly into my dream why should they come, p. 47

Temples, yes, there are temples, dung-coloured, p. 139
Terrifying are the attent sleek thrushes on the lawn, p. 73
The apes yawn and adore their fleas in the sun, p. 70
The bells of waiting Advent ring, p. 11
The cars speed up and down. Under the surface lie, p. 45
The celluloid of a photograph holds them well—, p. 67
The fat flakes fall, p. 123
The furthest stars recede, p. 119
The green light floods the city square—, p. 107
The hard blue winds of March, p. 111
The lighted city is dark, but somewhere a bus, p. 56
The month of the drowned dog. After long rain the land, p. 77
The pig lay on a barrow dead, p. 75
The road climbs from the valley past the public, p. 96
The shepherd on the fell, p. 38
The stars wheel past the windows, p. 120
The sun has set, p. 123
The sun has set; the curtain stirs;, p. 37
The toadstool towers infest the shore:, p. 128
The winter clenched its fist, p. 40
The winter night is round me like a skull, p. 126
'*The village inn, the dear old inn*, p. 8

There he goes, tacking against the fields', p. 149
There was Dai Puw. He was no good, p. 148
These are the ghosts of the unwilling dead, p. 88
These mountains of up-pointed spears, p. 136
They huddle in groups on shingle, aiming, p. 134
This Bantu on a bicycle racing the sunset, p. 137
This fossil in my hand, p. 46
This man swaying dully before us, p. 148
This thin elastic stick was plucked, p. 54
This was our valley, yes, p. 41
To live in Wales is to be conscious, p. 146
To make the best of Fate's inordinate demands, p. 93
Tonight the wind gnaws, p. 115
Treetops, spires and houses—all have grown, p. 140
Turning aside, never meeting, p. 149

Under the scarlet-licking leaves, p. 107
Up the ash-tree climbs the ivy, p. 3

We sail at dusk. The red moon, p. 131
We were a people taut for war; the hills, p. 146
When I returned from school I found we'd moved:, p. 12
When I was young, when I was young!, p. 143
When to the music of Byrd or Tallis, p. 19
White-arched in loops of silence, the bodega, p. 113
Who said to the trout, p. 152
Who were they, what lonely men, p. 37
Who's that knocking on the window, p. 20
Winter: winter in the woods, p. 59
With a jack plane in his hands, p. 52
With the ship burning in their eyes, p. 132
Woman, you'll never credit what, p. 101

'*Yes, I was only sidesman here when last*, p. 4
Yes, I know. They are like primroses;, p. 147
You are the old, the violent and melancholy master of that final land, p. 98
You have black eyes, p. 137
You served me well, Prytherch, p. 144
Your hair that makes the most of vines, p. 140
Your Irish wit made you bequeath, p. 46